# THE
# ATAVIST
# TAROT

THE

# ATAVIST
# TAROT

SALLY ANNETT   ROWENA SHEPHERD

## quantum

LONDON • NEW YORK • TORONTO • SYDNEY

# quantum

An imprint of W. Foulsham & Co. Ltd
The Publishing House, Bennetts Close,
Cippenham, Slough, Berkshire SL1 5AP, England

ISBN 0-572-02582-3

Printed in Great Britain by St. Edmundsbury Press, Bury St. Edmunds, Suffolk

# CONTENTS

For our children
Censi, Alice, Milly and Morgan

◆

Sally would like special thanks go to her
family, the Silbury Group, Ian Kuah, Venus,
the Benstead-Dallyns, Soraya Billimaria,
Sarah Wright, Legge Potter, Alex Mitchell,
Alison Thomas, the Kasers, Jessica Rost and
MKAA MK Community Trust Southern Arts.

◆

# 'Madness is purely conceptual.'

# THE FRONT PATH

## Introduction

♦

### The Magpie Song

One for sorrow
Two for joy
Three for a girl
Four for a boy
Five for silver
Six for gold
Seven for a secret – never to be told

## Sally Annett

As a child, I was raised in an Anglican/Christian culture. I attended schools where the Lord's prayer was said, took part in nativity plays at Christmas, painted eggs at Easter, and was sent with tins of fruit for harvest festival. I was read nursery rhymes that told me that women and children – from Cinderella to Thumbellina – are vulnerable, 'at risk', but that old, wise women are witches and evil. I was given a thousand and one visual stories, adapted aesthetically to my era. I understood none, and did not know which to believe.

My two great desires were to talk to animals and to fly. No one else, apart from other children, seemed particularly interested in these career choices. At five I wanted to be a nurse and have a husband. I still haven't achieved either of these goals. What I have are children – both the artistic and creative and the real human versions. They have become my life. Each child is equally demanding; and because there is only one of me, they are rarely sated at once.

Like Pope Joan, I wanted it all and I have learnt much in trying to achieve it. I have learnt most about my limitations. The formats I use to express my realities have firm limitations – each contained within a canvas stretched over four sticks of wood. Each is an investigation into an aspect of experience. I want to know. I want to understand. I want to see what the stories really mean, to find the one true story.

Christianity is right to say that there is only one God. In my opinion it omits to say that he has many names, many aspects, and that there are many ways to find God. So my paintings are very simple. They are my own personal investigation as well as being an expression of my reality with all its wild imaginings. I use theological and historical references;

I play with the information at my disposal. I follow my instincts utterly as I paint. The rules, the value judgements I make, are both fully conscious and arising from a deeper, more subconscious plane. I paint in an altered state, my focus wholly outside myself, absorbed in process and creation, but always tempered by experience or conditioning – by the physical.

This project is the culmination of both my and Rowena's lives so far (mere striplings that we are!). I am attempting to make sense of the complexities and abstractions of the world around me, and in doing so I stumble again and again upon archetypes and underlying similarities. 'The more I know, the less I understand.'

The Tarot was the natural vehicle for my work. The painting which focused the project was the Queen of Cups, and I started working on it a week after the birth of my first daughter, Censi. I had been painting wildly for years, but motherhood (the 'hood', a cloak of limitation) required a more disciplinarian and proactive approach. My time had gone; welcome to the collective!

My work in the previous nine months had been centred on very fat, seated women, and I decided to haul myself out of this gestative creative state. I wanted to construct an image that was distant, separate from myself. Setting myself an objective, a technical exercise, I chose ten cards from my Tarot deck, intending to create a narrative piece. But lo and behold, the cards, the images I was presented with, brought deeply personal images up from my own life to the point where I was almost embarrassed to allow people to see the work. I should not have been surprised that the Tarot cut through my conscious clutter to expose these underlying truths. That was when I wholly committed myself finally to painting a Tarot deck.

One year on, the Buckinghamshire County Museum Service asked me to submit an exhibition proposal for the works. Being pregnant again, I stalled and proposed a date at least two years later. It was purely by coincidence that the exhibition opened on Friday 13 February 1998. Due to the physical size of the work, the exhibition could only display the twenty-two paintings of the Major Arcana.

I approached Rowena in 1997 in the hope that she would write some accompanying text for the exhibition, and marvellously she agreed although she was pregnant at the time. Now we have made this book together, and have three daughters and one son between us.

# Rowena Shepherd

I feel the same as Sally in that this book was something I was given to do: a task in return for a gift. I have a similar upbringing to Sally and, like her, I am a self-taught Tarot reader. The Tarot provided me with a lifeline, a mother's voice after my adopted mother died when I was a teenager. They gave me a sense of the spiritual and mystical after I reached puberty and discovered that Christianity denied my right to have these things in an active and personal sense. Later, when I was at university, I took a course in my third year called 'Images of Women from Antiquity to the Fifteenth Century'. I took the opportunity to write my report on the images of women in the early hand-painted Tarot decks because I wanted to know about the origin of the images on the cards. My research answered some questions for me, but revealed the void history has placed around certain proscribed ideas and visual objects.

The creation of an image from the Tarot cards also sparked off this project for me. I was getting to know my blood mother by visiting her in Wales. Like me, she had interests in an outside spirituality and I was fascinated by an image of the goddess which she kept in her garden. Whilst I was in Wales, I took the opportunity to make my own goddess out of clay, copying the image on the Empress card. This was a signal to me that I had become seriously interested in the magical tradition. It also signalled that I subconsciously wanted to have a child with my husband, Rupert (who has helped me as much with the birth of this book, as with the birth of our child). For the next four years I studied the magical tradition with my mother, Helene Watson, and her good friend Michael Beechey; I also conceived a daughter.

In the summer of 1996 a friend's sister working at the Buckinghamshire Museum Service rang me up, asking if I would be interested in writing the text for a Tarot exhibition. I said I would, but thought no more about it because the opportunity seemed too good to be true. Then, the following summer, whilst I was pregnant with my daughter, Sally contacted me about her paintings.

I therefore see this book as the culmination of our personal exploration of the cards. For each of us it turned into something else when we created a physical image from the cards. Each of the images we initially created was an image of fertility and creativity. And thus, a gift was born and, as in any good fairy story, if you are given a gift by a good fairy, you have to do something in return.

# Sally and Rowena

Atavism represents the idea of inherited characteristics from the distant past. Both the deck and the book have been created in a way that builds up symbols, vision and ideas, reaching back into the innate oneness of humanity's past, and breaking through the barriers of disparate cultural and sexual identities.

We have felt that much of the time it is the Tarot itself that has directed us in this atavistic quest. So that whilst we both bring very separate skills to the project – Rowena being the writer and Sally being the painter – at this point it is difficult to distil out discrete elements. Because of the differences between our two disciplines, this book has benefited greatly from the careful editing and advice of Suzanne Gilbakian, who has pulled together the loose threads and shaped it into a consistent whole.

Sally and Rowena both wish to communicate similar philosophical and spiritual beliefs, which we are both aware are fully beyond ourselves as single individuals. We both do our utmost to support the other in engendering the form of the whole. Rowena uses words, conjuring with verbal visual images; Sally creates visual images that inspire others to use words.

What is most marvellous is that Sally created these Tarot images having known only the Crowley Tarot intimately. She has thus taken her inspiration from deep within herself and from a guiding force without. Likewise, Sally gave Rowena her images without commenting on what they meant to her. Thus Rowena had to work from her own reactions to the images without being guided verbally by Sally. The magical result is that we splice the one side along with the other, without artifice, without subtlety, yet it creates a complete whole. It comes full circle, it is the magic of the creative process.

Later in the book, we have examined and explained in more detail the genesis of the Atavist Tarot project and the evolution of this creative process. Most readers, particularly beginners, will want to work with the cards straight away and begin to become familiar with them, and those readers can move on to the next chapter, which illustrates a simple layout. A few readers, particularly the more experienced, may feel they would like to understand the development of the work before beginning to use the cards themselves or reading about the imagery of the Tarot; those readers can turn to page 229, then come back to using the cards at a later stage. Whichever route you choose to take, you will become familiar with a house of images which, when laid out in a particular schema, interrelate in such a way as to create resonances that provide clues to the narrative patterns within each person's life story.

# THE FRONT DOOR

## Meeting Your Tarot Deck

◆

## Your first layout

What most people want to do when they get a new deck of Tarot cards is to open up the crisp packaging and spread them out so that they are able to look at the images. The next impulse is usually to start using the cards. In acknowledgement of this, this first chapter is not a long explanation of how to use the cards or a description of their meanings (both of these will come later), but a description of a quick and simple spread so that you can begin getting acquainted with your cards straight away.

### Shuffling the cards

Hold your deck of cards in your hands and shuffle them as well as you can. If you wish, you can think of a question while you are shuffling the cards. When you feel that you have finished shuffling them enough, lay all the cards face down, spreading them out into a fan shape.

### Picking the cards

Pick eleven cards from the fan, without peeking at any of the images, but merely allowing yourself to feel for cards that 'feel hot' to your hand.

### Laying out the cards

Lay these eleven cards one by one, still face down, in the order illustrated in Diagram 1. Start with the position marked A and continue laying the cards down according to the diagram in alphabetical order.

### Turning the cards

When all eleven cards have been placed in the layout, turn over each card one by one, beginning with card A. As you do so, say the phrase following each card's letter aloud.

DIAGRAM 1.

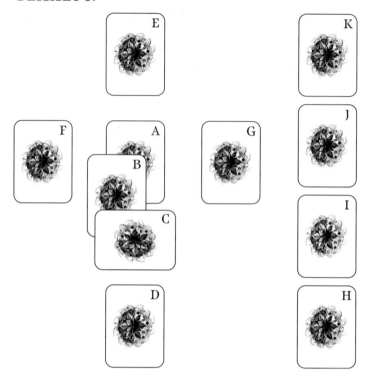

Turn over card 'A' saying:  **'This card represents me and my basic situation.'**

Turn over card 'B' saying:  **'This card covers me.'**

Turn over card 'C' saying:  **'This card crosses me.'**

Turn over card 'D' saying:  **'This card is beneath me.'**

Turn over card 'E' saying:  **'This card crowns me.'**

Turn over card 'F' saying:  **'This card is behind me.'**

Turn over card 'G' saying:  **'This card is in front of me.'**

# Interpreting the cards

Now, one at a time, look up the meaning of each of the cards (again, in alphabetical order) in the 'Study' chapter, on page 37.

You may wish to take notes of your readings or keep a Tarot diary or journal for later reference. The first three cards give an overview, or summary, of your situation.

### A  The significator card

This card represents you because you have shuffled the cards and asked the question. It also includes the psychological factors affecting you.

### B  The covering card

This covering card represents the basic situation and the outside factors affecting you.

### C  The crossing card

The crossing card represents the influences around you which are blocking the covering card – in other words, the external or internal obstacles or problems you are encountering at the moment.

The next two cards represent factors in the situation which you consciously and unconsciously bring to bear on the outcome.

### D  The past influences card

This card represents elements from your past which are unconsciously influencing the current situation.

### E  The expectations card

This card represents your conscious thoughts about the outcome of the situation in the future.

The last two cards represent events and people instrumental in the situation.

### F  The recent past card

This card indicates what events have happened and who has been influencing you in the recent past.

### G  The near future card

This card indicates the near future and events and people about to come into your life which will affect the ultimate outcome of the question asked.

This concludes the general narrative of events surrounding the outcome of the question asked. It covers what has happened and what will happen, as well as how you have been and currently are feeling about the situation. This is the basic story told by the cards.

The next set of cards to be read, referred to as the staff, tells you about your own internal reaction to the ultimate outcome.

### H  The self card

This card represents your internal self, your feelings and attitude to the outcome.

### I  The environment card

This card represents how you, and the question you have asked, are seen by other people. It includes the opinions of people around you – from family and friends, to your bosses and people you wish to influence.

### J  The hopes and fears card

This card represents your hopes and fears about the outcome. Often these are one and the same. For example, when you really want something, like a new job, you can also be afraid that you won't want it when it is obtained, or that you won't be up to carrying out the new responsibilities you will be given.

### K  The outcome card

This is the final card and represents the ultimate outcome of the reading. It indicates whether you will achieve your goal or will be given something you didn't expect. It is important to remember that you can always change the outcome. The cards only describe what will happen if you continue to act in the way you were acting before this particular reading.

Sometimes the outcome card is ambiguous. This is usually because you are not sure whether you really want what you are asking about. This card will reflect this ambiguity. There also seems to be a hidden morality in the cards where they will not tell you something you didn't already suspect. In that way, the cards cannot affect the ultimate outcome. Indeed, sometimes a card like the High Priestess appears in this final position, indicating that the cards cannot tell you what the ultimate outcome is at the moment. However, nine out of ten times the card in this position does reveal the outcome. When it does not there are ways of asking further questions to help you understand why the cards are ambiguous. (See the section of the next chapter entitled Furthering Your Reading on page 24).

The spread you have just used is called the Celtic Cross. It is the best spread to use for beginners and the most common way of divining with the cards. This spread provides a good general reading for answering most questions and is relatively easy to remember. This is because the position in which you lay each card visually represents its meaning.

We chose to start this book by asking you to lay out the cards, even though you may be unfamiliar with their meanings. This was because the easiest way to learn is by doing. However, you are still likely to have questions about laying out and reading the cards. The following chapter is intended to answer some of these questions. In addition, you will find that the more you use the cards, the more you will learn about how they work for you.

woman of dises

# THE HALLWAY

## How to Use
## the Tarot Cards

◆

### Shuffling the cards

Shuffle the cards for a few minutes. If you have a question, think of it all the time you are shuffling. Try to concentrate; if you are chatting about something else, that topic will get mixed in with the answer that the cards give you.

If cards accidentally fall out of the deck while you are shuffling, pick them up, look at them and then put them back in the deck. They will have a meaning related to the question you have asked.

It is difficult to explain how you will know when to stop shuffling. Most people stop when they feel ready. I stop when I get a prickly feeling in my fingers. When someone else has been shuffling the cards, I pass my hands over them when they are handed back to me to lay out. If my fingers start prickling, I know they are ready.

Other people have different methods of working out when to stop. Finding your own way of knowing when the cards are ready is part of the process of becoming a Tarot card reader. However, if you are unsure or not yet confident, there is another, fail-safe method: after shuffling, take the deck in your right hand and cut it into three piles. Then, again with your right hand, place the piles back on top of each other in any order, picking the cards from the top.

### Asking a question

The person who is asking the question should usually be the one shuffling the cards. However, if you have a question about someone else you can shuffle the cards and ask the question for them. Remember that the cards will always answer the question from the point of view of the person shuffling the cards.

Of course, you don't have to ask a question. If you are not sure what you want to know at the moment, the cards will simply tell you about the next most important event in you life.

However, if you do have a specific question, repeat it in your mind as you shuffle the cards. It also helps if you can visualise the situation that you are asking about whilst shuffling the cards. When formulating your question, think it through carefully; a simplistic question will not give the cards scope to give you a full answer. The following are some sample questions to help you formulate your own questions:

> If someone has come into your life and you are wondering what sort of relationship you will have with them, you could ask:

### What sort of relationship will I have with this person?

This is better than asking if you will fall in love with them or if they will cause you problems. In questions such as these you are already trying to predict the outcome within the question. You need to give the cards the scope to explain fully what the relationship will be, rather than limiting the cards to a particular answer.

> If you are about to start a project or a new job and you are worrying whether you will succeed or fail, you could ask:

### In what direction will this new job take me?

Again, this gives the cards scope to explain how the job will affect all parts of your life. We tend to see things very narrowly – work only affecting work, and home life only affecting home life – whereas in reality both are part of a single person's life, and one will affect the other. We also tend to see things as successes or failures, when in reality life is more complex. Every experience is a success, as it helps you to grow and understand yourself and the world around you.

> If you have a job interview or an exam and want to know if you will get the job or pass the exam, you could ask simply:

### Will I pass the exam/get the job?

Questions such as this will sometimes give you a direct answer, but more often they will tell you how the situation will affect your life. With direct questions it is better to use a spread other than the Celtic Cross. A shorter, more concise spread is illustrated on page 27.

If the cards don't seem to be answering the question, don't worry. They will often ignore a question if there is something more important you need to know.

# A sample Celtic Cross reading

This reading is for a woman who has recently had a child. She and her partner are living in a cramped flat and she wants to move. But because both their jobs are temporary, they cannot plan when to move or where to. So, 6
whilst visualising the issues worrying her, she asked the cards:

DIAGRAM 2.

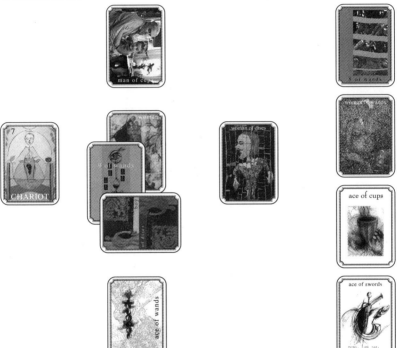

### How is my home situation likely to develop?
### The significator card
**Woman of Cups:** This card is a good one to represent the woman, as the Woman of Cups often represents motherhood. It also indicates that her motives in this situation come from her emotions and her wish to surround herself and those whom she loves with a loving and emotionally secure environment.

### The covering card
**Nine of Wands:** In this case the card shows how the woman's internal emotional desires are reflected in her

outside wishes, with the desire to break down the boundaries of her old life and grow beyond them. Although she expresses this desire by wanting to move home, she actually wants to make a greater change; she wants to move her life on as well. She feels that her physical situation is limiting her to her old life, and that moving will in some way allow her to be the new person she really wants to be.

## The crossing card

**Boy of Discs:** The basic meaning of this card is planning and developing an idea. However, because it is in the crossing position, it represents a block in this part of the questioner. As she indicated, she is unable to plan or arrange a move at the moment because of outside influences. This card also represents being rewarded for hard mental work, which suggests that she is relying on or waiting upon a reward that has yet to come. This may be in the form of either her or her partner getting a new, more permanent job, which will allow them to plan what to do next with their home.

## The past influences card

**Ace of Wands:** This position represents the drives and influences from the past subconsciously affecting the current situation. The Ace of Wands indicates that she has, in the past, been used to taking on a situation and transforming it into what she wants through the sheer force of her own will. That energy is still there, and she wants to use it in this current situation.

## The expectations card

**Man of Cups:** This position represents her ideals and conscious desires for the future. She desires a secure and stable family home where she is prepared to sacrifice her own needs to create the right environment for those she loves. She obviously has a very strong image of what a family home should be and what she as a mother should be. She feels that her current environment doesn't provide this.

## The recent past card

**The Chariot:** This card in this position indicates that she sees herself in the past as having prepared for the future, and that creating a family home is the harvest. She has obviously invested a lot in creating a family and a home. The advice given with this card is that although she appears to be in control of her aims and desires, there are forces beyond her control that are guiding her forward.

### The near future card

**Woman of Discs:** This card subtly indicates that she will get what she wants, as it represents being in a secure and happy environment. However, unlike the Four of Wands or Ace of Discs, this card does not directly indicate physical property or a new home. Instead, it reveals the hidden motives behind her external desires: she needs the home in order to find a place of rest to heal herself.

The Woman of Discs represents someone who has had a hard life, which has affected her physically and emotionally. In this case, the woman's mother died when she was a teenager. Her father could not provide the lost security because he too was hurt. So she took responsibility for her own life without direct support from others. This card indicates that she has been trying to get back to where she was before her mother died. She wants to create a family home so that she can start the healing process.

### The self card

**Ace of Swords:** This card represents someone using their intellect to think through problems. New ideas and great clarity of thought allow her to cut through internal and external problems to reach her goals.

### The environment card

**Ace of Cups:** This card shows that she has no direct enemies around her; people are loving and supportive. This is because to others she appears to be acting out of motives of love and generosity of spirit. She is already surrounded by the emotional security for which she has been longing.

### The hopes and fears card

**Woman of Wands:** She knows that she has the experience, creativity and emotional strength to carry out her visions. At the same time she is confused and afraid that the goal she has so longed for is not within her reach. She understands herself enough to recognise weaknesses in herself and she is afraid these are enough to prevent her from achieving her goals. All along she has felt that the death of her mother was in some way a personal judgement and that she is doomed to live without a secure home or family.

### The outcome card

**Five of Wands:** In her striving to create her dream, represented by the Man of Cups, she has taken on a lot of work and responsibility. As the Woman of Wands in the position of her hopes and fears indicates, she fears that she no longer has the energy to reach her goal. But in reality, she does. The Five of Wands shows that her weakness comes from a loss of focus. This brings us back to the crossing, or blocking, card (the Boy of Discs). Because she feels that she can't plan for her future, she has stopped planning or looking at things logically. She needs to stop and regroup, to take things one at time, and to spend some time planning out what she wants again. This self card indicates that she has the intellectual capacity to do this easily.

As the reading of the last card indicates, in order to read the story the cards are describing you often have to look at the other cards in the spread. It is important that once you have created the basic reading, you then look at the patterns and repeating motifs in the layout to get an idea of how each card links with the other. This is how it is done.

## Overview of the layout

### Major Arcana cards

Major Arcana cards hold more power than other cards. In this reading there is only one Major Arcana card, the Chariot. This gives a clue to what is driving the woman's aim of a harvest. It helps explain the underlying need this woman feels and which has caused her to ask the question.

### The aces

Ace cards are the next strongest as they indicate the energies available to the woman to help her achieve her goals. In this case she has all of the aces except the Ace of Discs. This helps to explain why she is expressing her needs in terms of the material. She is asking for a home – not love, new work projects or will-power. In other words, the lack she feels expresses itself in material terms.

When two or more Minor Arcana cards of the same number appear in a reading, their positions indicate the process of transformation of one energy or situation into another. In this case she has doubled her energy by transforming the energy of the wands and will-power into the double energies of mental and emotional strength. She needs both these energies now so that she can plan her actions for the emotionally secure future she desires.

## The court cards

The questioner has three women in her cards, representing the transformation process she is undergoing. Her emotional desires (represented by the Woman of Cups) are transformed via the Woman of Wands (a woman who has the emotional strength and creativity to carry out her visions) into the Woman of Discs (a woman with a secure and happy home) where she can root herself and start to heal her internal wounds.

## The minor arcana

This particular reading does not have a preponderance of one suit or another. However, a spread with significantly more cards of one suit than another usually indicates the problems are weighted on one side of the person's life:

**Wands represent the ego and confrontations with other people**

**Cups represent relationships and emotional stresses**

**Swords represent the intellect and coping with change or disintegration**

**Discs represent the material world and issues to do with work and material security**

I have found that when one suit predominates in a reading it often indicates the way that a person looks at life as a whole. For example, I have done a reading where a woman was dealing with a lot of emotional stress in her life. In particular, a lover from a failed relationship came back, looking to re-ignite their relationship on the eve of his wedding to someone else. The reading, however, instead of showing lots of cups, was full of discs. In this case the root of her problems came from the fact that she had put her emotional energies into the material side of her life. The love affair had been based purely on physical desire. And thus they both backed off, or made light of the situation, whenever it looked as if it was going any further. As a result, the emotional side of the relationship had never been properly worked through.

Another example turned up in a reading for a woman who was having problems with her husband. They were in financial difficulties and he was working very hard to keep the money coming in. To her despair, he kept on spending it on frivolous things, like gifts for her and going out and enjoying himself. The cards representing her husband were dominated by cups. This indicated that he thought about material security (and money in particular) in emotional terms. Seeing this helped the woman understand that her husband's fears of loss of material security were being expressed by using the little money they had to make her and himself feel happy and emotionally secure.

People often ask about the time span a reading represents. Minor Arcana cards can give an indication of when events are likely to happen.

| Wands | = Spring |
| Cups | = Summer |
| Swords | = Autumn |
| Discs | = Winter |

Where the cards are placed also gives an idea of progression and change. For instance, both of the arms of the cross in this reading show a definite progression in the events surrounding the woman.

The vertical arm of the cross (which is read from bottom to top) represents subconscious influences from the past reaching through into the present to create a conscious desire for the future. In this case, the drive or will (represented by the Ace of Wands) leads to the woman becoming a mother (represented by the Woman of Cups). This in turn leads her to desire a secure and happy home (represented by the Man of Cups).

The horizontal arm of the cross (which is read from left to right) represents events in the past that are creating the present and working through into events in the future. Here the woman has been preparing in the past for a harvest (represented by the Chariot), the fruit of which was the birth of a child (represented by the Woman of Cups). This allows her in the future to heal the wounds of the loss of her own mother (represented by the Woman of Discs). This, in turn, was the underlying driving force behind the Chariot.

# Furthering your reading

The simplest way to find out more about the particular meaning of a card is to pick another card and put it beside the first one. Listed amongst the divinatory meanings of each of the cards in this book are instructions for doing this, especially when a card is chosen that seems negative.

However, there is another, more in-depth, method of doing this. It is useful when a particular card just doesn't seem to fit the reading, or perhaps the questioner wishes to know more. This involves creating a miniature Celtic Cross around the card, using the problem card in the position of the significator.

The outcome card in the previous reading was the Five of Wands – a Minor Arcana card. This has the effect of making the reading conclude with a comma rather than a full stop. It is as if the question the person asked hasn't quite been answered. When part of the reading isn't clear or hasn't been explained properly or if you are simply unhappy with what it indicates, you can interpret the reading further by treating the card in question as the significator in a simplified version of the Celtic Cross. You do this by picking up the next card from the top of the pile and laying it across the problem card. You then pick four more cards, which you lay around these two cards in exactly the same way as you did for the cross part of the Celtic Cross. You miss out the covering card, however, as the significator will represent them both.

I continued the previous reading in this way, obtaining the cards in Diagram 3.

**DIAGRAM 3.**

### The significator card
**Five of Wands:** This card represents a lack of focus and having too many things to deal with.

### The crossing card
**Girl of Discs:** This card could indicate becoming pregnant again, but it is more likely to represent waiting for the message that will say whether she or her husband has secured a more permanent job.

### The past influences card

**The Universe:** This card represents the elements from her past affecting the present. It indicates a completion and achieving goals. In this case, it indicates the birth of her child and becoming part of a family again.

### The expectations card

**Fortune:** This card indicates that she wants to move onwards to something new.

These three cards together explain the outcome card in the centre. This woman has just experienced a momentous change in her life with the birth of her child. Yet instead of standing still and experiencing the joy of the present, she has lost her focus on the present. The only things which she can see clearly are her desires for the future.

### The recent past card

**Death:** This card indicates that a dramatic change has just been brought about in her life. The death of the old ushers in the new.

### The near future card

**Nine of Discs:** In the future she will experience life to the full, fulfilling her talents and, most importantly, sharing her experience of life with others.

This particular reading holds some very strong cards, as three of them are Major Arcana. The message of the cards seems to be that it is not the property this woman has that will fulfil her life, it is the sharing of her life with her new family that will bring about the peace and healing she seeks. The strong vision she has built up in her mind of how a family should live is disrupting her enjoyment of the real family she has. In other words, she has lost her focus on the here and now; she already has what she needs to be happy.

# A spread for a simple yes or no answer

The best spread for asking questions requiring a simple yes or no answer is this small pyramid spread as shown in Diagram 4. As with other readings, the significator card (card A) represents the person and their position in the situation being asked about. Card B represents their hopes around the situation, and card C their fears. Card D represents the influences from the past, and card E the present situation. Card F indicates the future, and card G what the overall answer to the question is.

This spread may seem too long for a simple yes or no answer, but I find that it helps to have a little context within the answer. In that way you can understand some of the basic forces involved in creating the answer. However, an even shorter way of answering a yes or no question is to simply pick a single card from the deck.

**DIAGRAM 4.**

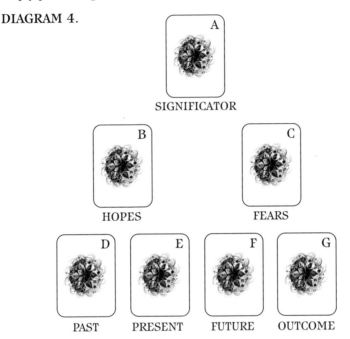

SIGNIFICATOR

HOPES          FEARS

PAST    PRESENT    FUTURE    OUTCOME

# A spread for a year

This is the largest spread I am going to show you (see diagram 5). It is also the most complex, but I have found it to be very good for getting a clear picture of the issues due to appear during the course of the coming year.

The position of the cards only gives a general indication of their meaning (such as the past or present). Moreover, each card is not given an individual name and none of the positions has a meaning other than where they are in relation to the past, the present, the future or the message of the cards. Therefore, this reading relies on the reader being able to intuit what the patterns made by the cards indicate. So this is really a spread for a more experienced reader. However, after trying the other spreads you should have gained an ability to see the patterns made by the cards and how they can be read. It should not be long before you are also able to use this spread.

To begin with, the cards should be put face down on the table. You first lay down the three S (significator) cards in chronological order: S1, S2, then S3.

Lay out the three past cards above the past significator card from left to right. Then lay the three present cards in the same way above the present significator card. Place the three cards representing the message of the cards above the future significator. Then lay out the near future cards, again from left to right. And last of all, lay out the three future cards beneath these three cards.

The groups of cards can be read in any way you like – left to right, right to left, or the card in the middle balanced by two outer arms. You have to use your own intuition to work out the narrative patterns.

**DIAGRAM 5.**

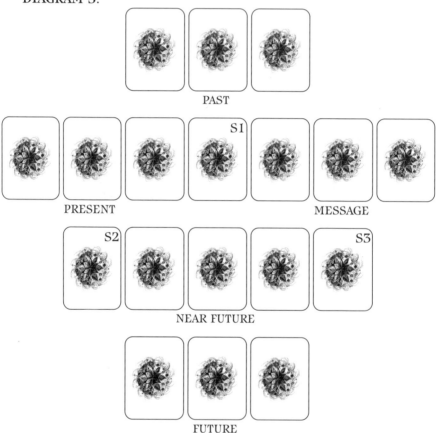

PAST

S1

PRESENT                MESSAGE

S2                S3

NEAR FUTURE

FUTURE

This reading was done for a man whose work contract was about to come to a close. Although he did not ask a specific question, he was worried about finding work again in the future.

# The Significator Cards

The first part of this reading is done by uncovering the three significator cards. These represent the questioner's feelings about the situation. They indicate the progression the rest of the cards will reveal.

These three cards can also give an idea of timing as well. In this reading the Seven of Discs represents winter and early spring, the Boy of Cups represents early summer, and the Man of Cups represents late summer.

DIAGRAM 6.

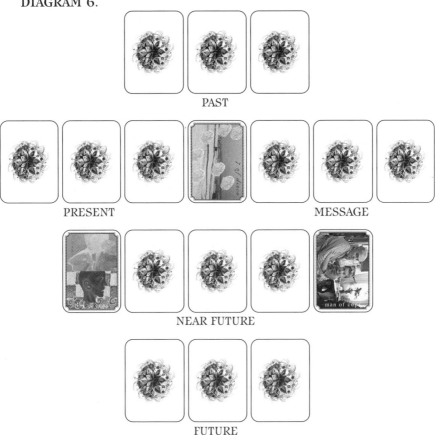

PAST

PRESENT                                    MESSAGE

NEAR FUTURE

FUTURE

Now follow the text and turn over the cards relating to past, present and future.

# Past

Having uncovered the significators, you now turn over the top three cards. Groupings of three cards can be read in anyway that seems to make sense. The important thing is to look at the significant cards to see if any pattern emerges.

Here the progression begins with S1, the Seven of Discs. This represents the past, a time when the hopes and fears of the questioner were bound up with material concerns. It moves to the present with S2, the Boy of Cups who represents youthful emotional desires. In turn, these desires develop into a more mature expression of love in the future, as shown by the Man of Cups in S3, representing emotional responsibility and family.

DIAGRAM 7.

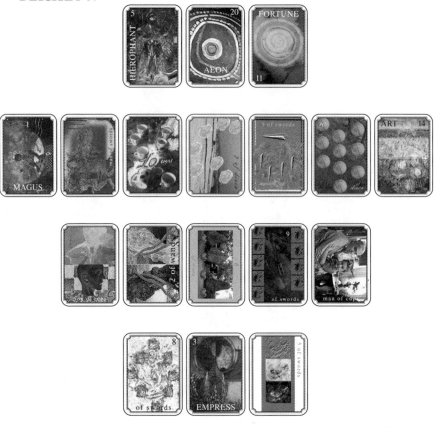

In this reading there are three Major Arcana cards above one Minor Arcana card. This indicates that major events are happening externally, affecting how the person feels internally. Major Arcana cards are always considered heavy cards and weight a reading towards their side. If the situation were reversed and the significator card was a Major Arcana card and the other three cards were Minor Arcana cards, it would indicate that the person's internal reactions were affecting external events. In this case, the events being described indicate that one phase of the person's life is coming to an end.

**The significator card – Seven of Discs:** This card represents the person's internal fears, especially the fear of failing. In this reading I have chosen to read the three Major Arcana cards from left to right. They indicate what was causing this man's internal fears and how he reacted to them.

**The Hierophant:** The position of this card indicates that the man initially listened to advice coming to him externally.

**The Aeon:** This is the card of leaps in understanding, and thus it indicates that the advice helped him to understand the situation and his fears around it better.

**Fortune:** This card indicates that as a result of seeing things through other people's eyes and conquering his fears, he moved the situation on. Thus, the next cycle of his life was able to begin.

# Present

The way I have just read the three cards of the past, from left to right, is not rigidly fixed. As the next cards will show, you have to have an eye for the patterns of meaning the cards reveal.

## The significator card – **Boy of Cups:** This card represents the internal feelings of the questioner; it indicates that this man has a tendency to repress his emotions and fears in order to appear externally strong. The card indicates that he does this because his emotions about the situation are extremely powerful. As a result, he has an underlying feeling of being trapped by life, and thus he has a compelling need to be in control. He also has intense dreams and ideas of how life should be.

**Man of Swords:** I have chosen to take the court card directly above the significator as the starting point for this particular reading, as it is a direct external expression of the questioner's internal feelings represented by the Boy of Cups. Externally the questioner appears to be in control: he is aggressive in his approach to life and acts in a focused manner. This man uses his mind to think his way out of problems.

**Magus:** The intellectual side of the Man of Swords is emphasised here by the Magus card. The questioner is able to communicate his ideas freely and to influence others into helping him create his dreams.

**Ten of Cups:** This card represents the emotional side of the significator card, indicating both outward and emotional success. This man's external material goals have a direct impact on his emotional well-being. In other words, he is capable of achieving his dreams.

# Message of the Cards

When reading this type of spread, you next turn over the message of the cards. This is because they often have a direct bearing on how you should look at the future. In the case of the message segment of this particular reading, the three cards can be read from left to right.

**Five of Swords:** This card appears to be leading on from the Seven of Discs next to it. The questioner is afraid of change itself and is thus paralysed by his fear, unable to make the move onwards.

**Ten of Discs:** This card indicates that the situation surrounding the questioner is actually quite a happy one. This man is blessed with many gifts and talents. He now has to transform his understanding of himself. In the past he has been used to taking and learning from others; but now it is his turn to give of himself and pass on his knowledge to others.

**Art:** This man's success is indicated by this last card. Art represents unity, above all a blending of gifts and knowledge. It also indicates becoming a channel for inspiration both to inspire oneself and others.

# Near Future

When doing a reading for a year, the next stage is to look at the near future cards. Unlike the past and present groups of cards, the significator is not read with these cards. Instead, it is used as an outcome card, representing the outcome of the progression described by the next set of six cards.

**Two of Wands:** This card represents the solid foundation this man has built for his future. His initial plans have been fulfilled and he is now ready to work out where he wants to go in the future.

**Six of Discs:** By taking planned risks this man can maximise the outcome of any venture. He has sufficient faith in his future to create the future and to fulfil his goals. Moreover, new opportunities will arise.

**Nine of Swords:** Despite the positive message of the last two cards, this man is being blocked by internal fears and lack of self belief. This blockage is coming through from the Five of Swords above this card, which in turn is feeding through from the Seven of Discs.

# Future

The final stage is to look at a broader picture of the future.

> **Eight of Swords:** In the future, this man will be presented with several choices – as a result, he will be afraid of making the wrong decision.

To clarify where help in decision-making will come from, I asked the questioner to draw another card. He drew the Four of Swords indicating that since he has built a solid foundation in the past, he will have the strength to win the battle in the present. However, this card also indicates that despite this, he has not yet won the war: more is to come. He will be given a period of rest in which he can distance himself from his immediate problems. In this way he will be less immediately attached to a particular outcome, and will be able to make the decision required by the Eight of Swords in the light of rational thought, rather than in the heat of the moment.

> **The Empress:** This card indicates that this man has the gift of creativity within himself and that all he touches will grow. He has the ability to fulfil his goals, a view reinforced by the Six of Discs.

> **Three of Swords:** This card indicates that he will still be holding within himself the fear represented by the Nine of Swords and that it will eventually resolve itself in grief. This will come about as a result of a bursting out of the emotions and fears he has held trapped within himself.

Because the Three of Swords seems negative in this position, I asked the questioner to pull another card. This turned out to be the Death card. At first this might seem to be another negative card, confirming Shakespeare's observation in *Hamlet* that 'When sorrows come they come not single spies. But in battalions'. Death, however, actually represents the ending of this man's fears, ensuring that he only experiences this level of grief for a short period, before other events quickly overtake the situation. Indeed, the very fact that when the ending comes, it will come quickly, is probably the reason this man is afraid in the first place. Fear of the unknown is at the root of most of our fears.

## The outcome card

> **Man of Cups:** This card represents a happy and fulfilled person. It also indicates that no matter what problems he might be experiencing now, the support to overcome them comes from his home environment and his family ties and relationships. Therefore, his stresses are not so strong that they threaten to damage what is most important to him – his home and the people he loves.

# Astrological spread or personality reading

DIAGRAM 8.

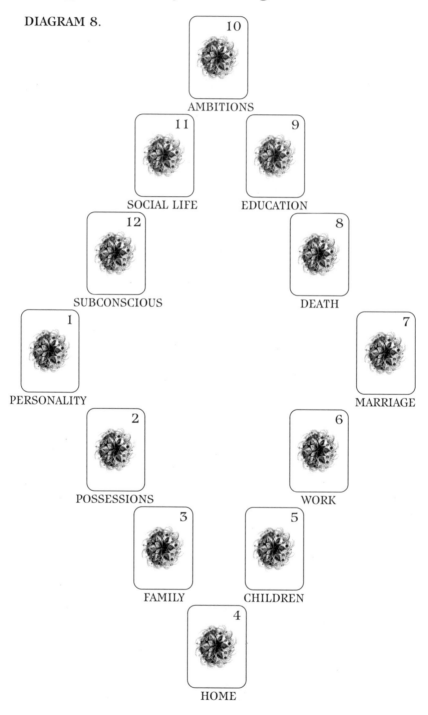

You need not limit the cards to answering questions about the future or personal problems; their use is only limited by your imagination. I would even encourage you to develop your own spreads. This next spread comes from the astrological houses that divide a person's birth chart. It can be used to reveal a person's basic motivations and their attitudes towards different areas in their life.

The method of working with this spread is slightly different than the others. This is because the positions in other spreads are more general, such as past or future, whereas the positions in this spread relate to complex ideas, such as personality (in position 1). You thus have to relate a single card (such as Ten of Cups) to the personality of the person for whom the spread has been laid. In this case you could perhaps describe a questioner as being very attached to emotional security and desirous of being in the centre of things emotionally and the emotional pinwheel around which the family and other social groups revolve. Such a person would be very giving with their love, which may sometimes appear smothering.

For instance, in position number eight, the house of death, you might have the Six of Swords. This would indicate that the questioner has had a visionary or transforming experience related to death and the life force issues, such as birth, death and sex. This would mean that as a result they have been transformed in the way they live their life. Another person might have the Girl of Swords in the same position, indicating that they have overcome their fears surrounding the issues of death, sex and birth, and that this has given them the courage to face difficult life situations.

## The meanings of the houses

**First House:** This card describes the personality or the outward appearance of the person to others. It also indicates the person's general health and physical appearance.

**Second House:** This card relates to possessions and the person's attitude towards these possessions. It can also include the questioner's level of income and their ability to keep or spend money.

**Third House:** This card represents the person's family ties. It also represents the person's experience of school life and their ability to express themselves intellectually in daily life.

**Fourth House:** This card represents the questioner's attitudes to their home, including any property or land they may own. It can also indicate attitudes to parents and emotional responsibility.

**Fifth House:** This card represents children and creativity. It indicates the sort of pleasures the questioner gains from life, especially in terms of love affairs and physical activities.

**Sixth House:** This card represents the questioner's work, and, to some extent, their physical well-being.

**Seventh House:** This card represents the questioner's close personal relationships, especially long-term relationships such as marriage or those formed with business partners.

**Eighth House:** This card represents the person's attitude to sex, birth and death. It represents both the life force and the darker side of the questioner.

**Ninth House:** This card represents the questioner's attitudes towards, and ability within, education – especially that of higher education and study. It also indicates travel abroad and attitudes towards foreigners.

**Tenth House:** This card represents the ambitions of the person, especially in terms of their career. It also indicates the attitude of the person towards responsibility and self-discipline.

**Eleventh House:** This card represents friendships and the person's ability to socialise or take part in a group. This includes shared objectives in the questioner's life and intellectual pleasures they derive from activities such as reading and art, as opposed to physical pleasures.

**Twelfth House:** This card represents the person's subconscious and their desire to escape. It also indicates how they cope with being alone with themselves.

# THE STUDY

## The Interpretation of the Tarot Cards

◆

## The Qabalah and the Tarot

The Qabalah has become a touchstone for understanding the mystical significance of the Tarot cards. The *Yetziratic Text* (Book of Creation), which was probably written in the Middle East some time between AD 100 and 600, is the earliest written version of what we now know as the Qabalah. By the late twelfth century, Jewish mystics in Languedoc and Spain further developed this concept, calling it Qabalah, or 'received lore'. They expounded it in the detailed text of *The Zohar*. It was this text that Christian Renaissance Humanist, Giovanni Pico della Mirandola (1463–94) used in his studies of natural magic, along with the hermetica. The form of Qabalah today used in conjunction with Tarot cards is a gentile version developed by the occult lodges of the eighteenth and nineteenth centuries.

In the same way that creating a divinatory layout provides a structure around which a narrative can be based, the method by which the cards can be laid out upon the Tree of Life (the visual glyph of the Qabalah) creates a narrative of correspondences with this complex mystical structure.

The Tree of Life consists of ten spheres, called Sephiroth, and the paths than run between them. In the Western occult tradition it is customary to memorise some of the basic meanings of the Sephiroth and their paths, and then to meditate on each of these. This is called path working. Meditation on the Qabalah starts from within to find both spiritual and material correspondences with the universe without. If we are each created in the image of God, we should be able to relate ourselves to the divine by working from within ourselves. We are in this way the microcosm relating to the macrocosm.

According to the Qabalah, in the beginning was the truth, the essence of God. It chose to take on material form, the *prima materia,* or prime matter. By doing so it created the first duality through the concept of existence and nothingness. Then, as this original matter shattered itself into infinite shards called the *primum mobile*, or first movement, and exploded outwards into infinity, time was created. All these things happened simultaneously. The Qabalah tells us that within each particle is the equivalent of a holographic image which belongs to the original essence and which reflects all that it was, is and will be.

# The Tree of Life

DIAGRAM 9.

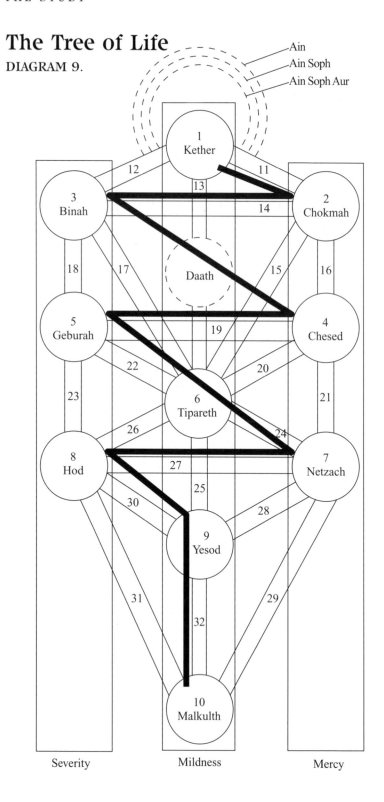

All this information is contained within the glyph of the Tree of Life. The act of creation is represented by the lightning that travels from Kether at the top to Malkulth at the bottom, and which is called the Path of the Flaming Sword. This is illustrated by a jagged line on the Tree of Life.

Above Kether are the three flaming crescents of the Ain, the Ain Soph and the Ain Soph Aur. They represent the mystical concept of the unmanifest from which Kether and all the Sephiroth below Kether arise. Each sphere and path on the Tree of Life relates to a letter of the Hebrew alphabet. The letters, in turn, relate to concepts such as the Godhead, the material world, the universe around us and our physical bodies.

# Meanings of the Sephiroth

| Number of the Path | Name of the Sephira | Meaning | The Principles of Creation | Experience of the Sephira | Aspects of the Self |
|---|---|---|---|---|---|
| 1 | Kether | the crown | first matter or the point formulated in the void | God the creator | |
| 2 | Chokmah | wisdom | divine fire, or the spark | masculine energy | the spirit |
| 3 | Binah | understanding | divine water, or the form builder | feminine energy | |
| | Daath | knowledge | Daath is the invisible Sephira, not normally represented on the Tree because it represents a bridge built across the abyss between the three upper Sephira and those below. | | |
| 4 | Chesed | mercy | the framework of manifestation | the builder | |
| 5 | Geburah | strength | the eliminator of the useless | the destroyer | the higher self |
| 6 | Tipareth | beauty | the redeemer | the healer | |
| 7 | Netzach | victory | nature | feelings and instincts | |
| 8 | Hod | glory | reason | the conscious mind and the intellect | the personality |
| 9 | Yesod | foundation | the astral level | the subconscious mind and dreams | |
| 10 | Malkulth | kingdom | the material universe | the body | |

The way in which these spheres relate to each other through the paths adds to the subtlety of meaning contained in this glyph, as does the way in which the structure is traditionally divided into three pillars.

# Three pillars of the Tree of Life

| Name of Pillar | Position | Colour | Qualities |
|---|---|---|---|
| Severity | left | black | female, passive, negative |
| Mercy | right | white | male, active, positive |
| Mildness | middle | grey | balances the other two pillars |

The Tree of Life also exists in what are described as four dimensions or planes. They are called the Four Worlds and they relate to the four letters of the Hebrew word for God (יהוה) known as the tetragrammaton.

# Four worlds

| Letter | Name | Level | Concept | Meaning | Being | Element |
|---|---|---|---|---|---|---|
| י | Atziluth | the archetypal world | essence of a concept | God form | God | fire |
| ה | Briah | the creative world | all the forms the concept has taken | archetype | archangels | water |
| ו | Yetzirah | the formative world | the interrelationships between concepts and matter | thought | angels | air |
| ה | Assiah | the material world | the tangible form of a concept | material | elementals | earth |

Additionally, in the *Yetziratic Text* the Sephiroth and the paths are placed in another diagram, called the Cube of Space. This was an attempt to link the Hebrew Tree of Life with the Pythagorean concept of the material universe, as represented by a cube. Although trying to link the two representations is problematical, to say the least, the Cube of Space is a useful concept to work with when using the ideas of the Qabalah for ritual magic. The division of the universe embodied in the Cube of Space can be recreated by magicians in the magical space in which they work. The different areas recreated can then be meditated upon, and their energies called upon during the ritual. Thus, the Cube becomes a physical way of addressing the energies of the Qabalah.

# The Cube of Space

DIAGRAM 10.

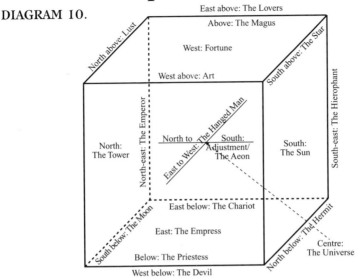

In this book, some of the following correspondences related to the Qabalah are listed after the interpretive text for each of the Major Arcana cards:

**Hebrew Letter:** The Hebrew letter related to the path.

**Meaning:** The meaning of the Hebrew letter.

**Yetziratic Text:** The description of the path given in the *Yetziratic Text*.

**Esoteric Title:** The esoteric title traditionally given to the path in Rabbinical literature.

**Alchemy:** The alchemical element, or concept, traditionally associated with this path. (This is only used in a few of the Major Arcana cards.)

**Astrology:** The astrological correspondence traditionally related to the path.

**Location in the Cube:** The position in the Cube of Space.

**Sound:** The sound given to the path in the archetypal world of Atziluth.

**Colour:** The colour given to the path in the archetypal world of Atziluth.

**Path on the Tree of Life:** The number of the path on the Tree of Life, and the two Sephiroth that it links.

There are additional correspondences (not all related to the Qabalah) listed for the four different suits in the Minor Arcana:

**Element:** The element traditionally associated with this path.

**World:** The archetypal world to which the suit is related.

**Energy:** The basic energy that is the drive behind the suit.

**Sexual Energy:** The sexual energy associated with the suit which describes whether the energy is male or female, and thus negatively or positively charged.

**Humour:** The humour related to each suit. The concept of the four humours originated in antique medicine, and was used up until the eighteenth century. Each humour is related to a basic personality type, and as such helps to describe the personalities behind the court cards.

**Quadruplicity:** The quadruplicity, which describes the individual's division into the physical, intellectual, emotional or spiritual.

**Season:** The season related to the suit, which can help give a timing to events taking place in the reading.

**Sephira on the Tree of Life:** The name of the sphere on the Tree of Life.

None of the Aces have been given an astrological or esoteric title correspondence. The Suit Cards have been given astrological correspondences. The Court Cards have been related to the four elements and have a further correspondence that does not appear in the Major or Minor Arcanas:

**Colour Scale:** Each of the four colour scales relates to one of the four worlds. The different Sephiroth are associated with different colours according to which colour scale is being used.

Because of the space allowed in this book, the description I have given of the Qabalah is neccessarily brief. If you are interested in finding out more about the Qabalah, more comprehensive studies can be found in books on to the subject. A few are listed in the 'Library' chapter (see page 243).

# THE MAJOR ARCANA

◆

## The Fool – 0

The sun is shining in the puddles. The Fool turns and looks at the blue purple mountains in the distance; they are huge and vivid against an icy sky. An eagle plummets in pursuit of a dove which seems almost to be teasing it. The jack is out of the box. Exhilaration floods through the Fool's heart. Bells jingling, he strides forward. Jumping the last few steps down on to the stone platform, he leaps, ecstatic, into the river...

The infant blinks its part-seeing eyes, unafraid and unknowing. The woman floats the wicker crib on the ripples, kisses the baby and pushes it out...

The fish sets off on its journey across the oceans. It swims its life away, leaping upstream against the current, becoming battered and bruised, to lay its young, the very spawn the river will wash far out to the sea...

### Keywords
REBIRTH – QUANTUM LEAP –
IMMENSE CHANGE – CREATIVITY –
RELINQUISH ALL FEAR – NEW BEGINNINGS

### Divinatory meaning
The Fool is a beginning, free from any limitation or control. It is starting out full of confidence. The world is unknown, and so fear is unknown. This card indicates that the questioner rejoices in the optimism of the innocent, believing that all they want can be attained.

Expect the unexpected. The Fool can mean the start of a new job or relationship, or even a new way of looking at yourself and the world. You are now daring to leap, where those with more experience might hold back. Life is too short not to try.

### Advice
Keep all realms of your life in focus – mind, body, heart and soul. Be confident. Don't look back, but reach out and hold on to the experience, trusting in the infinite wonder of the universe whatever happens! The Fool leaps in without fear.

### Question
What is the spring which has pushed you forward? Has it come from within you or from outside? Does it fulfill a desire or save you from a fear?

Draw another card from the deck to reveal more about where you are leaping.

## Concept of the card

A star-like mandala is in front of the image like a translucent doorway. Used for meditation, this mandala is the entrance to the universal subconscious, from which the cards gain their potency.

The Fool springs out of the box behind the mandala, like a jack-in-the-box. The cube box symbolises the material world – the place where the Fool's journey starts. Inside the cube is a room only just perceptible. It is an in-between place at the beginning of a journey or adventure, much like a cross-roads. The door in this room opens out on to infinite possibilities, inviting us to take on the Fool's quest and enter where angels fear to tread.

All of mankind is represented by the Fool in that we are only different from other animals because we have been blessed by inspiration from the gods. This perception of humanity is an old one, represented in medieval European literature by the Ship of Fools. Indeed, the saviours of humanity were described as being holy innocents or fools. Saint Paul, for example, described himself as a fool in Corinthians, and literature such as the legend of the Fisher King where Sir Percival is described as the holy fool.

The Fool on this card has breasts, indicating androgyny perhaps. This Fool may even be an old woman, reminding us that there is no fool like an old fool. Thus, the image makes us question our stereotypes. It emphasises that all roles apply to us – regardless of whether we are male or female, old or young. The Fool is a trickster, jumping out at us when we least expect.

The Fool is wearing the traditional black and white of the jester. This motley echoes the black and white floor beneath, both representing the balance of nature. Where there is light, there is darkness; yin needs yang; all is polarity. We have to tread equally on both the light and the dark during life. The black and white chequered pattern appeared on the backs of the earliest playing cards, made in China. This traditional pattern also reoccurred on some of the earliest Tarot cards.

The Fool's crescent-shaped hat resembling the shape of the moon suggests a balanced mind. Historically, the moon was considered a source of folly; one of her names, Luna, is the root of lunatic. This reminds us that madness is purely conceptual.

The Fool's path on the Tree of Life is called the path of aleph. The Hebrew letter *aleph* bears no sound; it is a silent carrier of vowels and therefore symbolises nothingness. It is from this nothingness that the universe, and everything in it, was created. The moment of creation is represented in this image by the spiral behind the Fool's head. This is a symbol for the spiral energy of time and it holds the energy that pushes the jack out of the box. It is an unstoppable force containing all those things that compel us to move forward in life, things that can be fearful or which can teach us wisdom. This force was often represented by the dog yapping at the Fool's heels in earlier Tarot packs.

The Fool is the spring that sets the universe in motion and on its journey. Thus, the Fool also represents the concept of time, without which change and difference are not possible. The Fool is like Adam and Eve after they have eaten the apple of knowledge and are able to understand the differences between things and recognise good and evil. As such, this spring looks like the underbelly of the snake which tempted them. It is no coincidence that infinite time is often represented by a snake curled round on itself eating its tail.

# Symbols associated with the card

✧ **Hebrew Letter:** *Aleph* א

✧ **Meaning:** The ox which pulls the plough

✧ **Yetziratic Text:** Fiery or Scintillating
Intelligence (Time)

✧ **Esoteric Title:** The Spirit of Aether

✧ **Alchemy:** Uranium and Air, or breath
of God which sparks creation    △

✧ **Astrology:** Uranus ♅

✧ **Location in the Cube:** Central axis

✧ **Sound:** E natural

✧ **Colour:** Bright pale yellow

✧ **Path on the Tree of Life:**
11th – Chokmah to Kether

# The Magus – 1

The child sits seriously studying the game. Play is no longer a trivial amusement; there are patterns, structures and pathways to explore through the game. There is love, art, money, God – which one to choose? Which game?

The child needs to remember all the rules for all the games. He remembers that he has to count for dominoes, and that there are sets, trumps, runs and flushes with cards. The child remembers the rules and grows more skilful in his matches, but still he does not win over certain opponents. Then he realises that there is a different game, called cheating, and that this game has its own rules and stratagems. Then he realises that he has a choice: there are after all better games...

## Keywords
COMMUNICATION – AMBIGUITY – POWER – ILLUMINATOR – MAGICIAN – MANIPULATION – DETERMINATION

## Divinatory meaning
The Fool is stepping out on a life-quest, and as the Magus he is taking the first steps. He thus represents the will-power to achieve your goals. You are at the peak of your mental powers and can bring your dreams to fruition – the trick is to set your idea in motion and allow yourself to believe in your goals. You need to remain open and flexible, juggling your ideas and skills. There is an excitement about you: you have the power to use communication to convince others of your ideas.

### Advice

Beware, for you might get what you wish for; be clear what the consequences of your actions will be, for every change will affect the world and people around you. Wishes can be like buses: you wait and wait and nothing seems to work out how you want it, then suddenly you find you are expecting the child you have been wanting, you are forced to move into the house you always wanted and you are given the work opportunities you have wished for – all at the same time. You are so busy coping with your blessings that you don't have time to experience and enjoy them!

### Question

What is it you wish for? Explore your wishes and think about what really makes you happy. It may help to write your wishes down so that you can study them in detail.

# Concept of the card

The Magus is seated on the other side of the Fool's mandala, the veil of the subconscious. He is a child playing dominoes with tremendous speed, creating a rhythmical clacking sound as the dominoes hit the table. This demonstrates the speed and cunning wit of the Magus, whose powers are those of the god Mercury.

The Fool card is the creation of time, the creation of change and difference, while the Magus card is the communication of knowledge using this newly created change and difference and using the vibrations which fill the universe. The waves on the shirt of the Magus, and elsewhere, represent communication through vibrations, sound and light and radio waves, from which words and images are born and broadcast.

Most games contain an element of chance. While playing them one tries to control the outcome by out-smarting fate. This is the essence of magic – working with, and second-guessing, nature. The Magus plays both magical games and games with magic.

The game board beneath the Magus is similar both to temple flooring and chess boards. The snakes on either side of the board are perhaps from a game of snakes and ladders, or Mercury's wand, caduceus. This wand is used is for conducting power from the heavens to earth. In the same way, the Tarot cards communicate universal truths to us, whether we ask them mundane questions about our work and loves or deeper questions. The Magus on this card deals us the Ace of Hearts, answering our questions on our own motivations and what is at the root of the universe.

The mandala behind the Magus's head creates a halo effect. He is also enthroned, the magical master of his realm, learning the art of transformation and the mastery of the elements. The four elements are hidden in the picture. The mandala, which is also the sun, is the element of fire; this rises over an emerging landscape, the element of earth; the blues beneath the round table represent water; and fish rise up from this water and turn into leaves blown about the sky, eventually joining two magpies to indicate the element of air.

Magpies are sacred birds, with a touch of the Magus about them. In Australian dream-time myths magpies revealed the sun. When the sky was so close to the earth that it not only shut out the light but forced people to crawl in the darkness, the magpies decided that if they worked together they could raise the sky to make more room to move about. With sticks they slowly lifted the sky, until everyone could stand upright. As they struggled to lift the sun higher, the sky suddenly split open to reveal the first sunrise. Overjoyed with the light and warmth, the magpies burst into song. Magpies have greeted the dawn in this way ever since.

The Qabalah relates this card to the house in which the spirit dwells, calling it the first key. The Magus is the builder of this house. He first builds it on the levels of the spirit and then brings it down to earth by manifesting it in his actions on earth. Thus he creates a path for the spirit to manifest in matter. The Magus builds the house through meditation using tools such as Tarot cards. This is only the first step. To be a true Magus, one must bring the spirit into one's everyday actions.

This card also contains a warning. The black diamond beside the Magus indicates that we must always be aware that man's ability to manipulate the elements can be used for evil as well as good. The energy of the Magus is like electricity for it can be used to energise our actions in everyday life; but when used without thought, this same energy becomes like lightning, not caring which route it uses to earth itself.

## Symbols associated with the card

✿ **Hebrew Letter:** *Beth* ב

✿ **Meaning:** House

✿ **Yetziratic Text:** Intelligence of Transparency (Conductor of Prophecies and Visions)

✿ **Esoteric Title:** The Magus of Power

✿ **Alchemy:** Mercury

✿ **Astrology:** Mercury ☿

✿ **Location in the Cube:** Above

✿ **Sound:** E natural

✿ **Colour:** Yellow

✿ **Path on the Tree of Life:**
12th – Binah to Kether

# The Priestess – 2

She sees from within, remembering all, hearing her inheritance internally. She has not forgotten the men and women from whom she was born, but she does not recall them. She has no need.

Bright and busy is the talk and laughter of her aunts, constant in the background. Her companion is a flightless swan whose presence she never questions. They have never spoken directly to one another. Yet he too is rarely silent. He tells what the fishes have been doing, what they have seen and heard; often he exaggerates to make things a little more interesting.

She needs no food, no heat nor any external nourishment to survive – she is her own life source. Some days it is so noisy that she must retreat from her window, close the shutters and sleep for years at a time.

## Keywords
INTUITION – INDEPENDENCE – SELF-CALM –
VISIONS – HIDDEN EVENTS – WISDOM

## Divinatory meaning
This card means that the answer to your question, or part of your question, is hidden to you at the moment. There is potential in your life of which you are not yet aware. It will soon rise to the surface and transform your view of life.

This is a time in your life when the material world seems empty and you are aware of the inner mystery of the world around you. Dreams bring hidden wisdom to the surface, and it can be a time when intuitive, creative and even healing abilities emerge. However, although the Priestess is driven by practicality rather than emotion, your ambition for material gain is weak. Instead, you are driven to bring balance and beauty into the material world.

### Advice
You are strongly intuitive at the moment. Trust your own vision of how things will work out, rather than other people's visions.

### Question
At this particular time your dreams and day dreams are likely to be more vivid, and will provide clues as to what is about to happen in your life. Do your dreams and day dreams involve people from the past? If so, they may be indicating that an aspect of your relationship with these people, or events involving them in the past, is about to be repeated. Perhaps you have been dreaming of people who are around you at present. If so, this can indicate a change in your relationships. It may point to hidden desires or fears you may have about these relationships. It may even indicate an event that is about to happen and which involves the people present in your dreams.

# Concept of the card

The Priestess is a revealer of mysteries; she is represented by a female shaman, at once both attractive and mysterious. She has rent the veil between the two worlds of life and death, night and day, male and female, and stands confidently between the two. To do this requires great sacrifice, and she straddles the abyss like Christ. Like the reaper Goddess Kali she holds a scythe and can control the dominion of the darkness; but in this world she only has stories and words as her tools, much as Christ had his parables.

The Priestess may look alone, but a careful look shows that she is supported on the shoulders of those shamans who have gone before her. This also represents the birth of those who will come after her.

The Priestess represents a balance between male and female principles, as she has integrated feminine and masculine wisdom. She is the wise woman whose words are both sought and shunned. Although her words have been hidden and made fearful, she is a being of love and balance.

She is both Priestess of the moon and the Moon Goddess. Her power is that of water, holder of emotion and memory and controller of the tides. On her right is a water container. This refers to the meaning of the Hebrew word *gimel*, which is associated with the path of the Priestess on the Tree of Life. *Gimel* means water container; and like the camel, she carries memories through deserts of time and it is these which give her strength.

Water is shaped by vibration, holding the memory of whatever touches it. An active element can be divided many times in a homeopathic tincture until there is only a trace remaining and yet still be potent because the water enfolds it, holds it and retains its image or memory. This memory then vibrates through the whole substance.

The Priestess card is a card of memory, both racial and universal. This memory can be physical as well as mental. Physical memory is genetic; at birth you come into the world with knowledge, which would seem miraculous if genetic memory did not exist. An infant is able to recognise shape and form without having touched it first; a smiling face is attractive to the newborn. This genetic memory comes from our ancestors and makes sense of the universal existence of ancestor worship. As such, this card represents intuition and instinctive drives.

The conscious impulse to pass on memories separates us from other animals; we have the ability to pass on skills through communication and to store ideas through writing. Passing memories down through the generations allows the human race to develop and evolve, not merely physically, but allowing us to control the evolution of our own environment. This marks a progression from communication, without which memory cannot be transmitted from generation to generation.

Our memories contain fragments of the stories of the disappeared goddesses, resurfacing as fairy tales, the stories of apocryphal female saints and in our dreams. Once, we could reach them through day-dreaming or meditating. In the West our ancestors and vanished goddesses appear to us in our sleeping dreams. Dreaming whilst asleep is rare in the cultures where meditation or conscious dreaming still exist as part of everyday life. The Aborigines in Australia, for instance, regularly meet their ancestors and the gods in their dream-time travels. These lost goddesses are depicted on this card, their empty temples represented by the empty room to the right of the three seated figures. The swan-like figure on the left at the top is Leda, the goddess Jupiter loved whilst in the form of a swan.

In the middle top are three seated figures. These represent the hidden feminine trinity or the three graces, the maiden, mother and crone, the three phases of the moon, and the alchemical trinity of mercury, salt and sulphur. Beneath them are figures skipping, children whose games are passed down from one generation to the next. Their rope becomes the horns of the goddess Diana above the head of the Priestess. If you look carefully you will see that the rope is not being held by any of the figures but that the two handles are bees. This represents transforming joy.

In our paternalistic societies the female side of experience of divinity is often hidden or demonised; the language used to describe it is often dark and mysterious. Therefore, in our time she appears as both a warrior and a priestess, reclaiming her world.

# Symbols associated with the card

✦ **Hebrew Letter:** *Gimel* ג

✦ **Meaning:** Camel

✦ **Yetziratic Text:** The Uniting Intelligence (Memory)

✦ **Esoteric Title:** The Princess of the Silver Star

✦ **Astrology:** Moon ☽

✦ **Location in the Cube:** Below

✦ **Sound:** G sharp

✦ **Colour:** Blue

✦ **Path on the Tree of Life:**
   13th – Tipareth to Kether

# The Empress – 3

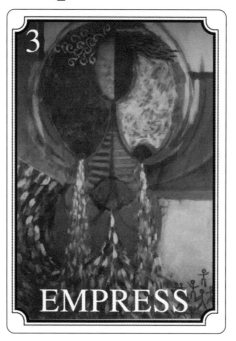

She combs her hair as her mother did; from the ends first, gently, but quickly untangling the fine threads. She stands, tall and slender, but strong like her great grandmothers before her. She stares at herself in the mirror and admires her ever swelling abdomen – continuity. She blinks, one eye blue and one brown, and turns to dress.

## Keywords
EVOLVING THE FEMININE – MATERNAL – SELF-SACRIFICE – LOVE – UNITY – FERTILITY

## Divinatory meaning
The Empress represents being aware of beauty and love. It is a time of passion and emotion, but also a sense of vulnerability. The card represents growth through the emotional side of your personality. The card is ruled by Venus. Therefore, women with this card in their readings are at their most attractive and men with this card in their readings find themselves attracted by women. The Empress also represents a generally fertile time of your life, and as such can sometimes indicate pregnancy. This card often represents the fertile ground in which the cards surrounding it grow.

## Advice

Take the chance to be in touch with the beauty of the creative emotions within yourself. Regardless of whether the passions you feel are sexual or imaginative, all you touch blossoms.

## Question

What areas of your life are currently being enriched?

# Concept of the card

The Empress is Mother Nature, the fertility goddess in all her forms. This card represents the possibility of creation and fertility, of bringing forth life and light from the darkness.

The Empress is the duality of nature. Without darkness, light cannot exist; in the creation of life is the seed of death. All material forms are subject to the forces of entropy through time. The goddess on this card shows Mother Nature's dual side: she is both light and dark, she causes famine as well as plenty. The circle around her head reminds us of the circular nature of life, of its growth, destruction and renewal.

The Empress, like Venus, represents fertility and the sexual side of the feminine, while the Priestess, like Diana, is the virginal side of the feminine. Hence, this card places emphasis on the reproductive organs, which pour forth the energy of life: from the breasts flow the milk of life and from the womb the menstrual blood of creation.

The Hebrew letter associated with this card, *daleth,* means door. The womb is the entrance to life from heaven, where the spirit is clothed in material form before birth. It is the cauldron of life in pregnancy, but it is also the place of the lesser death as the womb lining entropies during each menstrual cycle. The passage the child takes from the womb to the outside world is the most miraculous and dangerous it will ever encounter. However, even birth is a form of death. It represents the death of the parents' individual identities, as the child becomes part of their life. For the parents, birth is as traumatic an experience as the death of a loved one.

Venus, the goddess of childbirth, remains the goddess of love and sexual desire, for the womb is not only the cauldron of birth and formation, but also the male temple of hidden pleasure and desire. Within this paradox is contained the mystery of Mother Nature. Her breasts are offered both sexually to a lover and as essential food to a helpless baby – and she can deny the desire for both. This power to both give and withhold nourishing sexual and maternal love is at the heart of the male fear of women. Love and pure emotion are part of the essence, the illumination and the illusion of life and death.

The Empress is Eve. On the Tree of Life this card is on the path between Chokmah and Binah. Traditionally this is seen as the path where the female principle of Binah is created out of the male principle of Chokmah. The Empress of this deck has her ribs emphasised, reminding us of the story of the creation of woman from the ribs of the man, although both science and common sense would argue that this happened the other way round. This card represents the creation of the sexes, the separating out of male and female.

Binah's first form is as the great sea goddess Mara, the bitter mother. On the path on which the Empress card is placed, between Chokmah and Binah, energy is transformed from the one to the many, and thus becomes Mother Nature. The waters of the sea are separated out, creating the element of salt, the earthy element of the sea. This magical transformation is described in the story of the birth of Venus, who rose naked on a scallop shell from the salty waters of the sea. Wherever she trod on land, flowers grew which can be seen as the creation of the first life in the salty water of the sea and its evolution on to land. It is no coincidence that the amniotic fluid of the womb is salty and that new-born babies smell of the sea. Alchemically this card is linked with salt, which is used as a purifying element.

The features of the Empress contain within them the paradox of race. The white face has the curly hair and facial features stereotypically associated with black skin, while the black face has straight hair, blue eyes and European facial features. To Mother Nature these characteristics are practical, resulting from the conditions in which each race has evolved. Cold and dark or hot and light, she holds within her the features of both. The most recent understanding of genetic history shows that we all have common ancestors from Africa who are likely to have been black. The amount of genetic difference needed to produce either set of features is smaller than that between neighbours in a street: within us we hold the genetic possibility of either. We are all related nineteen generations back.

As the Empress represents duality and paradox, we find behind her the basic geometrical building-blocks of space: the circle and the square.

# Symbols associated with the card

✡ **Hebrew Letter:** *Daleth* ד

✡ **Meaning:** Door

✡ **Yetziratic Text:** The Illuminating Intelligence (Mother Nature)

✡ **Esoteric Title:** The Daughter of the Mighty Ones

✡ **Alchemy:** Salt ○

✡ **Astrology:** Venus ♀

✡ **Location in the Cube:** East

✡ **Sound:** F sharp

✡ **Colour:** Emerald green

✡ **Path on the Tree of Life:**
   14th – Binah to Chokmah

# The Emperor – 4

The Emperor is patient yet angry, wise yet a clown; he sifts and settles his power in layers and fissures. Loving and generous, whilst controlling and ever-hungry, he must battle with his conscience and tread kindly forward.

## Keywords

EVOLVING THE MASCULINE – LEADERSHIP – AUTHORITY – CREATING POWER STRUCTURES – ADVENTURE – HEED THE COLLECTIVE

## Divinatory meaning

This card represents your most basic feelings towards authority – both your own and that of other people. It indicates the need to order your life and take on responsibility for yourself. It is your fear of being constrained by hierarchies. The Emperor can signal an encounter with society's symbols of authority such as the law or government. It can also signify a person you allow to hold great power over your current situation; often this will be a father, or those whom you use as father figures, such as bosses, friends or lovers. Sometimes it represents the need to organise one's life rationally and create stable foundations, to defend one's social territory.

### Advice

This is a time when you can either stay put and feel secure within your current life situation, or break out and take a new direction, leading the way for others as well as for yourself.

### Question

Do you feel constricted and want to break out? What is the cause of your constriction? Is it blind anger? If it is, wait a while and then make your move. Do not domineer or bully to achieve your goals.

## Concept of the card

The Emperor on this card is a strong, ambitious man, crowned and seated on a throne, his legs open and solidly placed. He symbolises the attributes of strength, solidity, stability and matter. He makes and enforces the rules; he creates the mental structures through which the world is seen. He is reason and constructive logic, whereas the Empress is instinct and duality. The Empress was the creation of life and death, and the Emperor is the creation of the laws and hierarchies which govern our perception of nature. He is Adam, Cain and Abel; he is Zeus.

The Emperor's jacket is made up of defined abstract structures, which mirror his trachea, lungs and heart and which fit together like a jigsaw puzzle. This reflects the way in which he sees the messy and chaotic structures of nature. The Emperor creates the laws of science and the social laws of man, simplifying and demystifying the chaotic and powerful instincts that exist in nature, making sense of the senseless and creating the foundation on which the conscious version of reality exists. He wears the Fool's trousers patterned with lozenges, showing that temporal authority is not omnipotent for its origins lie in human society. Like King Canute, he cannot control nature, and this is indicated by the throne's human legs.

The Hebrew letter *heh* means window. This is the aperture through which man frames his understanding of the world outside or the aperture through which light and air come to illuminate the darkness inside the house. In the *Yetziratic Text* the Emperor is called the Constituting Intelligence, or he who constitutes the substance of creation in the darkness of the world. To constitute is to make something up from its parts, to structure, to compose; thus he is the builder of society out of nature. What he builds is his choice, for good or for bad; he represents the free will of mankind over nature.

The man on this card holds his child, representing the relationship of a father with his children. The path of the card is between Chokmah, the father, and Tipareth, the child. The Emperor sits relaxed and yet protective, the wise father, possessing and guarding his future. He represents societal and material inheritance. If his consort, the Empress, is Mother Nature, the Emperor is Paternal Society. This is a concept strongly at odds with our era. He is paternal society developed as a structure in which power could be passed down to the next generation through men's families, the creation of hierarchies through societal evolution rather than nature's genetic evolution. This is reflected in the phallocentric language of our current world.

To enforce social hierarchies, battles need to be fought. This card is astrologically related to Aries, which emphasises the courageous and warlike demeanour of the Emperor. The child he holds in his arms wears a white jacket, an innocent pure lamb, relating him to the childlike aspect of Aries.

Alchemically the card is linked with sulphur, a burning element associated with fire, and which, conjoined with Mercury, creates gold.

# Symbols associated with the card

✡ **Hebrew Letter:** *Heh* הי

✡ **Meaning:** Window

✡ **Yetziratic Text:** The Constituting Intelligence
(Structured Society)

✡ **Esoteric Titles:** Sun of the Morning –
Chief among the Mighty

✡ **Alchemy:** Sulphur ♄

✡ **Astrology:** Aries ♈

✡ **Location in the Cube:** North-east

✡ **Sound:** C natural

✡ **Colour:** Scarlet

✡ **Path on the Tree of Life:**
15th – Tipareth to Chokmah

# The Hierophant – 5

The quiet love of this being is born out of knowledge. He is the gradual evolution of form and light. He is difficult to see, impossible to photograph accurately. Whilst the Priestess is asleep he sings to her of ages past and secrets of spirit lost to the worlds of science and history. He is slowly developing a shape of his own.

## Keywords
**LIGHT – GUIDE – INNER VISION – TEACHER – SUBCONSCIOUS – INNER CENTRE – WISDOM**

## Divinatory meaning
Now is a time when you have access to your spiritual side. You have a need to find a spiritual teacher or path. This card can also symbolise higher education, and an alliance with those whose teachings you respect. It may also warn you that you are being too dogmatic with a particular view of life; this will be symbolised by the cards around the Hierophant. It can also indicate a tendency to surrender responsibility to other people.

### Advice

Listen to those you respect, and learn from them; but only believe your inner voice, not those of others. Seek the light within.

### Question

Is there someone around you whose ideas you are following at the moment? Keep your distance. Look inside yourself for the truth – it will ring as clear as a bell when you find it.

# Concept of the card

The name Hierophant is derived from the Greek *hiero*, meaning sacred, and *phantes*, meaning to show; it thus means revealer of the sacred. A Hierophant was the initiating priest in the Greek Eleusyian mysteries.

He is represented on this card by an abstract figure hidden in the scintillating colours of light which emanate from his centre. The painting has many layers, representing the process of initiation, a gradual process to reveal the whole. The figure is robed and, from his solid stance and muscular upper body, he appears to be masculine. His head is low on his shoulders and is horned. He is a Minotaur with a man's body and a bull's head.

The card is related to the astrological sign of Taurus the bull. In the same way that the Emperor is the foundation of society, the Hierophant is tradition and religion, the earthly foundation of spirituality.

Taurus is linked with the throat and speech. On many versions of this card in other Tarot decks two priests are shown kneeling before the Hierophant, listening to what he says. This is because the Hierophant is the Logos, the word, the inner voice, the written word of God, doctrine. The planetary influence associated with Taurus is Venus, and the bird sacred to Venus is the white dove, which also signifies the Holy Spirit or the divine presence as a voice.

As well as being secret doctrine, the Hierophant represents initiation into the doctrine itself, the process of being taught a religious tradition. He is the paternalistic side of the Priestess. Where she is visual intuition and memory of the ancient mysteries, he is the written and preached word, the traditions of religions and initiation into a structured spirituality.

The Hierophant has a rigidity to him, a rigidity we now associate with religious doctrines which enslave the masses and do not allow for individual thought. But as Tarot author Rachel Pollack points out, we should remember that all doctrines and traditions contain the essence of the deep mysteries. Many great mystics have spoken from within the ranks of doctrinaire religions rather than as individualistic outsiders. You need to understand the grammar of a language before you can communicate your unique inner visions, so the traditions of spirituality provide a foundation through which inner mystical visions can be expressed.

The meaning of the Hebrew letter for this path on the Tree of Life is nail. This path represents the nail that joins inner spirituality with outer doctrine. It is the path to an inner awareness of God in our outer understanding of the world. The idea of union is thus important to this card. On the highest level it is the true union of the personality with the higher spiritual self, or the union of the disparate parts of ourselves with the one true self.

On the Tree of Life this card is the path between Chesed and Chokmah and it is represented by a bridge over which the word of God flows into the world of religion. Another name for the Hierophant card could well be the ancient Roman title Pontifex Maximus, the bridge-maker and head of the state priesthood.

The artist has hidden on the four corners of this card the four sacred beasts: the lion, the angel, the eagle and the bull. These represent the four evangelists, the four elements and the four beasts described in Revelations as being seated around the throne of God. Also hidden in this card is the Tree of Life of the Qabalah. The orb between the bull's horns is Kether, the level of God; the central orb with the rainbow light of wisdom emanating from it is Tipareth, the Messiah; and between the Hierophant's legs is a shield with a red cross upon it, representing Malkulth, or the level of the material world.

# Symbols associated with the card

✡ **Hebrew Letter:** *Vau* ‎ו

✡ **Meaning:** Nail or hook

✡ **Yetziratic Text:** The Triumphal or Eternal Intelligence (Union with the Word of God)

✡ **Esoteric Title:** The Magus of the Eternal

✡ **Astrology:** Taurus (fixed earth) ♉

✡ **Location in the Cube:** South-east

✡ **Sound:** C sharp

✡ **Colour:** Red-orange

✡ **Path on the Tree of Life:**
16th – Chesed to Chokmah

# The Lovers – 6

At 10 she stood a foot taller than him
At 15 she decided she loved him eternally
At 15 he could not decide whom he loved
At 20 she remembered the gap he had left
At 20 he decided he loved her too
She changed her mind
At 25 she had children, not his
At 25 he had money
At 30 they passed in the street
Turned back and kissed for the first time

## Keywords
DUALITY – CONNECTING – LOVE – COMPLETION –
PARTNERSHIP – PERSONAL GROWTH – BALANCE

## Divinatory meaning
This card means a partnership; it may be a partnership of
love, friendship or work, depending on the question
asked. How this relationship affects your life depends on
its position in the reading. If the card falls in a position in
the past it can mean an obsession with a partnership now
dead that you need to move on from.

The card can also mean balancing of different sides of your personality, an embracing of the paradoxes within yourself. It can mean having to make a choice between two options – both equally attractive, but opposite in their effect on your life.

## Advice
Now is a time in which your internal and external barriers can be lowered. Nature's balance is love, so make your choices with your heart. Be sure to love yourself before attempting to love others.

## Question
What choices lay ahead of you? What do you seek for fulfilment?

# Concept of the card

This card is astrologically associated with Gemini, the twins, suggesting duality and balance. Duality and union is the nature of the universe. It is found in the sexuality of animals and plants; in energy (hence Newton's Third Law of Motion describing how for each action there is an equal and opposite reaction); and at subatomic level, with the attraction of negative electrons to positive protons.

On the Tree of Life this card is the path of Zain, the Disposing Intelligence. Robert Wang has revealed this path to mean הדגש *ha-regesh* – ה means the ד is the sun, נ the moon and שׁ is fire. Thus the image on this Tarot card is a combination of the Sun, the Moon and Fire. The man on the card is white and represents the daytime and the sun; the woman is black, representing the dark night and the moon, which is emphasised by her crescent-shaped earring. Together they hold and balance around the fiery orb of love.

As the figures of the lovers pivot around the light they are distorted into the shape of a balancing children's toy. If one figure was to pull away, they would both fall. The haloes around their heads join together in the centre to create a green flame. Green is the colour of Venus, goddess of desire and love.

The fiery orb represents the power of divine love, the initiating part of which is sexual love and desire. Zain means the sword. It is the flaming sword of love and desire, which pierces the armour of the self and unites rather than divides. When a couple unite in the act of sexual love, each conscious discriminating self is conjoined with the lover's subconscious desires, resulting in the death of their surface personalities during the sexual act. This union can only be fully undertaken within the heat of the fire of sexual desire, and it is around this fire that a relationship at first pivots. As the relationship between the couple continues, the breakdown of the surface egos also deepens. The fire of love thus changes until both partners are transformed and the couple become one to the outside world, finally joined in marriage.

This card is on the path between Binah travelling to Tipareth. This is the path of the sacred love of mother and son; it is marriage of the animus and the anima of the seeker. It can also be the union of the conscious self of discrimination (at the level of Tipareth) with the subconscious self of imagination (at the level of Binah).

# Symbols associated with the card

✧ **Hebrew Letter:** *Zain* ז

✧ **Meaning:** Sword

✧ **Yetziratic Text:** The Disposing Intelligence (Duality)

✧ **Esoteric Titles:** The Children of the Voice
 – The Oracle of the Mighty Gods

✧ **Astrology:** Gemini ♊

✧ **Location in the Cube:** East above

✧ **Sound:** D natural

✧ **Colour:** Orange

✧ **Path on the Tree of Life:**
 17th – Binah to Tipareth

# The Chariot – 7

It is the beginning of the new year, the snow has begun to melt and the smell of saddle soap and wood oils permeates the camp. The storers go into the woods to dig up the jars and sacks they had planted at the end of the harvest – large terracotta vessels stuffed with mushrooms, grains, fruit, berries, herbs, liquors, oils and spices. Meanwhile fires are being quelled, linen is being folded, pots, pans, tools and tack are all being put into their compact, but rightful, places. The animals are untethered. The horses are padded and harnessed, and children are loaded in the front of the waggon. There is a great clapping of hands. An intricate medley of singing, whistling and shouting erupts. The first footstep is as near as the last, as they head north – through spring and into summer.

## Keywords
CHANGE – PREPARATION FOR HARVEST –
UNSTOPPABLE – POSITIVE THOUGHT –
TRANSFORMATION – ACTIVITY –
IMPROVEMENT – BUSTLE – PROGRESSION –
ORGANISE – REVISE – IRREVOCABLE

### Divinatory meaning

The Chariot is the card of confidence and victory of the will. It indicates the ability to control a situation and overcome difficult obstacles through the force of your personality. It signifies moving from one phase of your life to another, harvesting the growth from one stage and moving on to the next.

### Advice

You need to prepare yourself for all possible outcomes. If you have prepared yourself, then all will change for the good. Although this card signifies a situation in which you appear to be in control, you should acknowledge that there are forces beyond your control guiding you forward. Tell yourself that you are putting your life in order and preparing for a new beginning.

### Question

Preparing for a new beginning can mean leaving things you love behind. Is what you are aiming for worth the sacrifice? Make sure you provide yourself with the support you need when your life changes. This is especially important where relationships are concerned.

## Concept of the card

The illustration on this card is a disembodied head enthroned by the wheels of a chariot, which is pulled by a bull-unicorn. The bull-unicorn represents the will, pure in its desires and determined in its progress. The head is disembodied because it represents the conscious mind, separate from the physical and the subconscious. The eyes of the head are closed with concentration: it is willing the chariot forward rather than commanding it physically, thus representing triumph of the ego over the self.

Astrologically this card is linked with Cancer, who is ruled by the Moon. So behind the Chariot is the pale shape of the moon, whose energies can impart intuition and clarity of thought when used positively, or deception and confusion if the actions are done selfishly, without openness and communication.

The Chariot is on the path from Binah to Geburah on the Tree of Life. This is called the Path of Influence, where the elemental levels influence the physical. It is a path of increase where those who have worked hard and prepared the ground can expect to harvest their victory. The charioteer carries with him an apple and a leaf which, with the grapes hung from the forehead of the beast, are a symbol of the harvest for which he has been preparing.

Underneath the Chariot is a wave of blue, representing the waters of Binah. The triumphant warrior of Geburah glides smoothly along these waters in his chariot, into the future and on to victory.

The meaning of *cheth*, the Hebrew word related to this card, is a fence or enclosure. Like the body of the Chariot which protects the charioteer as he moves through space, an enclosure can be a protective boundary to a garden or sanctuary, much as the shell of the crab (Cancer) is protective of the inner self.

A fence can also be restrictive and a prison. Thus, the enclosure describes the way in which the mind defines and perceives its surroundings. Within this description is a warning that the world, as envisioned by the mind, may not echo reality. When the mind cannot cope with the outside world, it sometimes creates a protective barrier around itself to keep out reality, seeing itself totally separate from the subconscious, emotions or the spiritual self. The mind can lose touch with reality and become arrogant and ambitious, imprisoned in its own view of reality. This card therefore warns against believing that material power and status are the touchstones of humanity and the salvation of the self.

An important lesson here is that although the mind and the will are powerful magical tools, they should be used with one's eyes open, with the understanding that sometimes, when one gets what one wills, it may hurt others and oneself. Hence the credo: 'Do what thou wilt, as long as it hurts no one.'

# Symbols associated with the card

✡ **Hebrew Letter:** *Cheth* ח

✡ **Meaning:** Fence or enclosure

✡ **Yetziratic Text:** The House of Influence (Victory)

✡ **Esoteric Titles:** The Triumph of Light – Child of the Power of Waters

✡ **Astrology:** Cancer ♋

✡ **Location in the Cube:** East below

✡ **Sound:** C sharp

✡ **Colour:** Amber

✡ **Path on the Tree of Life:**
18th – Binah to Geburah

# Adjustment – 8

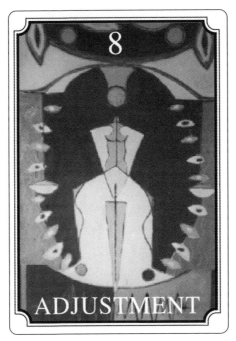

The driver of the first waggon is a short, hefty woman. She walks with a roll, her hips worn out from years in the saddle; this will be the eleventh time she has brought the nomadic tribes into their summer home. She leans forwards, elbows on her knees, face open and focused. She seems to steer the train effortlessly, without thought; but her body is never still, her arms constantly adjusting, steering, restraining and supporting the leather reins. Her legs bounce on the wooden footplates as she leans from side to side, constantly readjusting her weight, while anticipating every stone, every pothole and judging the angle of every slope and turn.

She loves the journey, the changes in the seasons and landscapes and the testing of her skills. When they arrive, instead of being exhausted, she is delighted and calm, full of purpose.

## Keywords
READJUSTMENT – JUSTICE – CONCENTRATION –
A TEST – SEARCH FOR TRANQUILLITY –
BALANCE – KARMA

### Divinatory meaning

The essence of this card indicates a balancing of your inner self in relation to your actions and the world around you. It is a karmic judging of the way you and others have acted. Depending on the card's position within the reading, the situation surrounding it is being judged.

This card often appears when changes are about to take place and will balance out what you have so far seen as unfair. Remember that although the outcome may not be what you expect, it will be fair on the universal level.

On a mundane level, Adustment may mean an exam or interview, or even an encounter with an authority such as the law. More generally it applies to having constantly to readjust to life's challenges and changes.

### Advice

During life, the aim is to keep the inner scales constantly balanced. In order to do this, you need to find your own centre point or pivot. Thus, this card calls you to search for your own point of inner stillness in the situation in which you find yourself.

### Question

You have recently been tested by a situation. Do you think you managed to find the middle path through it? What have you learned from the experience?

# Concept of the card

Originally this card was called Justice, but Aleister Crowley pinned its meaning down more accurately, calling it Adjustment. It is a depiction of the equilibrium of nature and is thus associated with Libra. On the Tree of Life this card is found on the 22nd path of twenty-two paths and is thus related to all the other paths, controlling the emanations from Kether in all of them. As the path's letter is *lamed*, ox-goad, it is also connected to the letter for the Fool, *aleph*, the ox or the path between Kether and Chesed.

The image of this figure of Adjustment is a complex composite of the Goddess Maat, the sword of justice and the arrow of truth. At any one time you may see one aspect more clearly than another. The way you see it at any one point may tell you something specific about the reading.

In Egyptian mythology Anubis holds the scales, weighing the soul against a feather. This feather was called the Goddess Maat, who was also the maker of the law and goddess of truth. She later evolved into the Roman goddess of justice, a statue which still stands above the Old Bailey, the central criminal court in London. The conjoining of the feather and the sword makes an arrow, representing the swiftness of justice.

Justice is usually depicted holding a sword, to mete out punishment or cut off the parts which weigh down the soul. The sword belongs to the

Geburah part of the path and the scales to Tipareth. In effect, we are being measured against the golden light of Tipareth, which represents the purity of the Messiah and the light of truth. The goddess Maat belongs to Tipareth, as she was also the daughter of the sun god Ra; hence we see the solar disc beneath the feathers in the illustration on the card.

The sword of Geburah removes the shadows in the golden light given off by Tipareth, providing the adjustment needed for our souls to travel up the tree to the higher levels. This is the philosophy of karma, where the Lords of Geburah justly mete out a sentence for our actions. The Hebrew letter for this path is *lamed*, which means the ox-goad that prods the Fool forward on the evolutionary journey. According to Paul Case, it also means 'to teach', hence the instructive aspect of the laws of karma.

On a more elemental level, the zigzag lines beneath the figure of Adjustment represent the tracings of machines measuring the vibrations of life such as earthquakes or heartbeats. This illustrates how nature adjusts the rhythms of life: for each pulse in, there is a pulse out. These pulses are the life-force emanating from Kether. In animals this is the body's autonomic system. It silently keeps our organs functioning, measuring the needs of our bodies and causing our organs to provide for these needs. It makes our hearts beat faster as we run and causes the placenta in the womb to provide for the exact requirements of the growing foetus. The Gaia hypothesis holds that the planet as a whole works in exactly the same way.

## Symbols associated with the card

✧ **Hebrew Letter:** *Lamed* ל

✧ **Meaning:** Ox-goad

✧ **Yetziratic Text:** The Faithful Intelligence (The Regulator)

✧ **Esoteric Titles:** The Daughters of the Lords of Truth – The Ruler of the Balance

✧ **Astrology:** Libra ♎

✧ **Location in the Cube:** North to south

✧ **Sound:** F sharp

✧ **Colour:** Emerald green

✧ **Path on the Tree of Life:** 22nd – Tipareth to Geburah

# The Hermit – 9

She sits huge within the city. People, cars and cables trespass through her, her enormity making her apparently invisible. She does not move despite the sprawling conurbation shifting throughout her. She has children, tiny spirits who play near or sit beside her, all surrounded by light. She is a gigantic inner angel, potentially so bright, but rarely seen. Close your eyes and look within.

## Keywords
DISCOVERIES OF INNER WEALTH – RESILIENCE – RESOLVING CONFLICTS – INNER GUIDE – SELF-SUFFICIENCY

## Divinatory meaning
The Hermit card heralds a gift of wisdom and maturity. It often represents a period in life in which you have to retreat from the everyday world in order to learn and study. Thus, it can mean taking on a course of study or retreating from sensual and materialistic goals in order to follow more spiritual ones. It is the urge to learn. If the cards around the Hermit indicate the influence of another person, it may involve listening to or being guided by someone older or more mature.

### Advice

You are being given an opportunity to create yourself anew: be aware that you can always learn. Now is the time to resolve problems from the past which are stopping you from moving towards the light.

### Question

What wisdom do you seek? Close your eyes and look within.

# Concept of the card

Traditionally the Hermit is a wanderer in the desert, whose solitary nature brings forth wisdom. The Hermit withdraws from the world outside in order to seek divine wisdom from the inner voice, often represented by the light from a lamp which he holds.

This card is related to the astrological sign of Virgo, representing the pure virginal aspect of the Hermit. Virgo also represents fertility and the earth, and so, as the Hermit wanders in the barren desert, he carries the possibility of new life. He is also the word uttered in a vast desert: the divine fire which fills men's hearts, an ecstatic spiritual experience of oneness with the inner self. Even though many of the early Christian hermits were women, the Hermit depicted in Tarot decks is usually represented as an old man. The age of the figure is important because it is a symbol for the older self.

The Hebrew letter for this card is *yod*. It is represented by a single stroke of the pen and thus is the foundation from which all the other letters are built. It is the essence of the word, or Logos, the divine fire of God. This card also symbolises a new beginning since *yod* is shaped like a sperm. Moreover, the sign of Virgo is the receiver of the sperm. This heralds a beginning of life, an opportunity to become a new person. The seed which fertilised the Virgin Mary entered through her ear. It is the inner voice or word that fertilises the spiritual self and represents the act of union between the higher self and the personality.

The woman in this card is shaped like the letter *yod*. She represents the mother pouring wisdom on to the child sitting in her lap. Instead of being in a desert, she is in a city overlooking the countryside. Here the desert is the mundane world around us; it signifies that we can be in a city and yet be alone.

*Yod* also means hand, an open hand rather than a closed one. Open hands are a sign of greeting and blessing and, most importantly, of giving. In this sense the Hermit is the hand of God, the execution of the supreme will, the urge to reach out to spiritual heights.

The Hermit is the way-shower or guide inside us all. Einstein's theory of relativity proposes that time is not linear, but curved. Thus, we exist at all stages of our being at one and the same time. The Hermit represents the flashes of inspiration that come from our higher selves when our mind is fertilised by wisdom from our older selves and when we understand the present in relation to both the past and the future.

In our old age we are the parents to ourselves as children. Thus, this card is interlinked with the Fool card. The Fool is the wisdom of our youth and the Hermit is the wisdom of our old age. This link between the two is a completion of the self.

# Symbols associated with the card

✿ **Hebrew Letter:** *Yod* ׳

✿ **Meaning:** Hand

✿ **Yetziratic Text:** Intelligence of Will (Wisdom of the Higher Self)

✿ **Esoteric Titles:** The Prophet of the Eternal – The Magus of the Voice of Power

✿ **Astrology:** Virgo ♍

✿ **Location in the Cube:** North below

✿ **Sound:** F natural

✿ **Colour:** Yellowish-green

✿ **Path on the Tree of Life:** 20th – Tipareth to Chesed

# Lust – 10

She stares at him as he lies sleeping, his breath slowing from rasping gasps to barely discernable flutters and sighs. He seems vulnerable. The curtain shifts in the breeze, making her pulse slam hard through her veins. With a childish grin, she steals across the room and out. Fearless now, she runs across the courtyard to the stables, and in minutes she is cantering off towards the river, through ferns and willows, unable to suppress wild shrieks of laughter.

Now she is tumbling from the beast's back, wriggling out of her clothes and into the water. As she swims she thinks she glimpses two figures on the far bank, but when she looks again, they are gone. The deeper water is warm. From the cloudless sky droplets start to fall, each creating crystalline explosions in the moonlight. She lies on her back and floats for a while. The rain stops.

She doesn't notice how she returned to the room, or what the time is, but he is awake. He has made her a hot drink and some toast. She smiles at him. 'Tomorrow if it's fine, you might like to come with me.' His face lights up. She chuckles inwardly picturing herself kissing his sleeping face before slipping out of the open door. She can never wake him, no matter how hard she tries.

## Keywords
**LIFE – CREATIVITY – STRENGTH – JOY – VISION – PASSION – EXPERIENCE – AWARENESS**

### Divinatory meaning

You find a new passion for life from within; ride this passion. Use it to find the strength to cut through the problems and obstacles you have been afraid of dealing with; you will wonder why you ever worried about them. Nothing good is done without passion; but remember that passion alone cannot create good work. This card can also indicate a passionate love affair, depending on the other cards around it.

### Advice

You will feel successful because of your new passion for life – riding high and seemingly endlessly creative. There is a warning contained in the next card, Fortune, that pride comes before the fall. Do not give yourself to passion. Remain the rider in control and be aware of where the passion is taking you. Use your new-found courage to defeat your fears.

### Question

What areas in your life have you been afraid to explore? What talents have you mistrusted and not used?

# Concept of the card

The card of Lust is astrologically associated with Leo, the lion of the stars. The lion is a proud and fierce animal, the king of the beasts. Lust represents the animal energy of the fierce beast and the anger and passion within us. It is also related to fiery energy and the Cherub of Fire. This cherub is found in the path of Geburah and is traditionally depicted as a lion with a man's face. Both the Cherub of Fire and the lion are creative energy, firing the path on the way to Chesed, the path of the builder or architect. Geburah is the destroyer and Chesed the builder, and this paradox engenders the creative lust which can either destroy or build.

Passion is not intrinsically an evil force, any more than a lion is an evil beast. It can be a positive and creative life-force, as well as a frenzied and blind destroyer that needs to be ridden rather than subjugated. Without the Dionysian passion of Lust, life would be empty and dull; man could never reach the divine heights of ecstasy.

The seven-headed lion depicted on this card and the attribution of it to Lust rather than Strength comes from Crowley's understanding of the energy behind this card. He represents the lion as the seven-headed beast of the Apocalypse ridden by the scarlet woman. This comes from his own personal belief that God can only create good and that behind the greatest evil is the greatest good. Thus, the beast is not only passion, but love; the woman riding the beast is not only desire, but virginity. The lion of passion can only be tamed by spiritual desire. The seven heads on both Crowley's lion and the lion illustrated in this deck are an angel, a saint, a poet, an adulteress, a daring man, a satyr and a lion-serpent. These imply that the lion represents the creative energy of passion and vitality experienced by all the heads.

At her most destructive the scarlet woman is the Whore of Babylon; she rides the lion, but does not subjugate it. In some depictions of Lust a woman is opening a lion's mouth, rather than closing it. She thus releases the energy of passion and controls it through the force of her will. The lion of Lust is not tamed or domesticated; he still contains the possibility of violence and destruction. His passion is controlled so that it becomes creative rather than destructive. The lion is a difficult animal to ride and the power it represents can become overwhelming if not controlled by the will. In this way Lust is similar to the Queen of Wands in that it equates experience with compassion, strength and wisdom.

Alchemically this card is also related to the image of the red lion, a symbol of sulphur purified and sublimated by mercury, or will. This signifies the mastering of one's own emotions or desires.

The Hebrew letter for this card is *teth*, the snake. Thus, Lust is connected to the idea of the serpent's power, the universal life force illustrated in the Magus card. The serpent's energy is the lust for life and it is this energy that is used in kundalini-yoga. The sign of Leo is associated with the sun, which governs the back, heart, sides and spinal column. These are the traditional yogic centres of power. The sign for Leo also resembles a snake.

# Symbols associated with the card

✡ **Hebrew Letter:** *Teth* ט

✡ **Meaning:** Snake

✡ **Yetziratic Text:** Intelligence of All the Activities and Spiritual Beings (Passion and Courage)

✡ **Esoteric Title:** The Daughter of the Flaming Sword

✡ **Astrology:** Leo ♌

✡ **Location in the Cube:** North above

✡ **Sound:** E natural

✡ **Colour:** Greenish-yellow

✡ **Path on the Tree of Life:**
19th – Geburah to Chesed

# Fortune – 11

Your eyes close, you start to spin forward down tunnels of light. Neurons in the brain rip vortexes in infinite space. Firework pulses, cables of light, atoms, electrons, quantum tunnelling particles, carbon and light. Accelerating through complex labyrinths and mazes of consciousness. Putting together the pieces. Do not panic: miracles happen all the time.

## Keywords
COMPLETION – AN ENDING – PROGRESS – KNOWLEDGE – GIFTS – MIRACLES

## Divinatory meaning
One phase of your life has finished and another is beginning. Be ready for sudden changes in direction. Fortune symbolises a breakthrough in the blocks and frustrations you have been experiencing; it heralds moving forwards again. Look at the cards surrounding this one to work out what the changes may be. This card can also mean gaining a fortune, on whatever level that might be – materially, emotionally or spiritually. Fortune may signal the end of a love affair or the beginning of a new job.

## Advice

Be ready to clear the decks, for you have a chance to start anew. The value of your shares can go down as well as up. Thus, you may experience losses as well as gains.

## Question

Are you ready for a change in what fate has to deal you?
Are you ready to be rewarded?

# Concept of the card

Fortune is traditionally depicted as a wheel on which mankind eternally rises and falls, spun by the goddess Fortune. When we are low we are pulled up, when we reach the summit of our powers we are then pulled down. Fortune represents the spiral forces of nature, the turning of the galaxies, the spinning of the planets and the uncurling of the leaf. It is the state of universal equilibrium and perpetual motion, the energies released in the zodiac, a wheel on which the twelve signs of the year rotate.

The existence of Fortune relies on the universe constantly changing. Without change there can be no fortune, either good or bad. Fortune is the motion of life itself: birth, death and rebirth. It is the wheel of karma upon which we reap what we have sown in our past lives.

Astrologically this card is associated with Jupiter, the controller of the circulation of the blood and the lord of Fortune. Jupiter denotes wealth and good fortune. The card is also called the Intelligence of Conciliation and Reward. Thus, after the finishing of this cycle, the next cycle will contain the conciliation or reward for the last. Hence, Fortune is the card of karma.

The card of Fortune in this deck depicts a spiral force contained within a band of equilibrium. The blood-red background resembles the womb and the spiral resembles the ovum. It appears as a pearl pulsating outwards or as the shell of an ammonite growing and constantly evolving.

The ovum has to divide and change in order to grow. Where the Hermit is the sperm, Fortune is the ovum. The Hebrew letter for the Hermit, *yod*, is the open hand, long and thin like the sperm. The Hebrew letter for Fortune is *caph*. *Caph* means a closed hand and is round and tight, like the ovum. The open hand gives, whereas the closed hand receives.

The card of Fortune marks the half-way point in the Major Arcana. The first half is complete and Fortune starts the new half. Thus, the ovum of Fortune represents the start of the next life, after the ending of the last. On the cube the card of Fortune is placed in the west, where the sun sets as the earth rotates. This card therefore means the completion of a cycle as we move on to the next day.

# Symbols associated with the card

✿ **Hebrew Letter:** *Caph* כ

✿ **Meaning:** Fist

✿ **Yetziratic Text:** Intelligence of Conciliation and Reward (Change and Completion)

✿ **Esoteric Title:** The Lord of the Forces of Life

✿ **Astrology:** Jupiter ♃

✿ **Location in the Cube:** West

✿ **Sound:** A sharp

✿ **Colour:** Violet

✿ **Path on the Tree of Life:** 21st – Netzach to Chesed

# The Hanged Man – 12

He had been there for four and a half hours. He had queued in line with his ticket, finally being evicted. His trade, his wife and family, his car, his stereo and his house – all gone. Today he has nowhere else to be. He is the genuine welfare article.

The room stinks; everyone can smell themselves and each other. They are all anxious, irritable and bored. Another hour and now his number comes up. He shuffles into a room with a woman who smells of hand cream, peering mistrustfully over a sheaf of paper at him. She coolly informs him that suitable accommodation has been found for him, dangling two small keys deliberately in front of him. At last, a gift, a way out, has been offered. He takes the keys and stands up, noting further forms to complete. As he turns to leave, she stands casual and distant as ever. Then she catches his hand and asks if she might take him out to dinner.

## Keywords
STALEMATE – DESTROYED PRECONCEPTIONS –
POSSIBILITY FOR COMPLETE TRANSFORMATION –
RELEASE – REALITY

## Divinatory meaning

This card represents the calm after the storm, a time in which you see things differently. Allow yourself to take a step back and wait for things to happen rather than making things happen yourself. The Hanged Man signifies a letting go of past angers and fears, and thus a release from worry. It can also signify the end of a troubled situation or relationship.

## Advice

If you are caught in a difficult situation in which there appears to be no way to win, let go and willingly sacrifice your own desires or point of view. In this way you can become a channel for light in a dark place.

## Question

Are there areas in your life with problems that don't seem to make sense? Do people have attitudes towards you that seem to be irrational? Can you understand these problems or people better when you look at them from a different angle? Draw another card from the deck to find a positive way through your problem or to discover what will happen when you tackle this problem.

# Concept of the card

The figure of the Hanged Man is suspended by his head in a trance, representing the suspension of personal consciousness, or the ego, in favour of the collective consciousness. This suspension or sacrifice has to be willing in order to gain spiritual transformation. So, the figure has tucked up his feet behind him so that he does not touch the earth. He is consciously cutting himself off from the world.

The internet and television are the closest we have come to making the collective consciousness real. Both are where the ideas, dreams, thoughts and beliefs of humanity materialise, and like the astral levels, they are conductors of consciousness. They receive ideas from a nebulous centre which does not exist physically.

The Hebrew letter for this card, *mem*, literally means seas. On the Tree of Life it is on the pillar of water, going from the water temple of Hod to the fire temple of Geburah. It represents a baptism in maternal water or immersion in the collective consciousness.

The card of the Hanged Man, as well as being a baptism, is also a crucifixion. It represents the idea of the dying God, a powerful myth existing in many cultures as Christ suspended on the cross, as Osiris killed by his brother, chopped into pieces and thrown to the corners of the earth, and as Odin suspended on the World Tree. In each myth, the sacrifice is made so that a transformation can be achieved.

This transformation is the ability to see things anew. Other versions of the card represent this by hanging the man upside-down, so that his view of the world has literally been turned upside-down. Another name for the card can be The World Turned Upside Down.

The transformation in this card is illustrated in the dual nature of the figure: he is both black and white, light and darkness. The Hanged Man is able to understand both sides. He represents the tolerance and understanding derived from immersing oneself in the collective consciousness. This allows one to reverse one's point of view totally in order to understand how other people think and feel.

The Hanged Man represents an openness to the world, without beginning or end; hence, it is called the Stable Intelligence. It is as if the wheel of Fortune has stopped turning and one is living in the stilled moment, which lasts for an eternity.

The card also represents awareness of God's support, holding us eternally. It is this support that gives us the freedom to let go totally, to release ourselves from the bondage of human ambition and troubles and to stop looking at life as a wheel of Fortune. Instead, as the Hanged Man we realise the desire to become a conductor of the universal spirit. The hands of the Hanged Man are long and fluid: they have become fleshy conductors of the universal will. They say: 'Not my will, but thine.'

The Hanged Man card symbolises transformation of our life. It is as if we become soul-naked and willingly sacrificed in order to transform our way of thinking. This leaves us free to receive the fiery inspiration from the collective consciousness, represented by the flaming bowl suspended at the Hanged Man's lap.

# Symbols associated with the card

✡ **Hebrew Letter:** *Mem* מ

✡ **Meaning:** Water

✡ **Yetziratic Text:** The Stable Intelligence (Transformation through Calmness)

✡ **Esoteric Title:** The Spirit of the Mighty Waters

✡ **Element:** Water ▽

✡ **Astrology:** Neptune ♆

✡ **Location in the Cube:** East to west

✡ **Sound:** G sharp

✡ **Colour:** Deep blue

✡ **Path on the Tree of Life:**
23rd – Hod to Geburah

# Death – 13

For every action there is an equal but opposite outcome.

The first time she is pregnant she dreams of white wolves. They chase her beloved deerhound, demanding a life for a life. She awakes weeping. Within a fortnight she has lost the baby.

For months she dreams of being bitten by snakes; she flees these nightmares repeatedly. Then one night she is pursued in her sleep to the sides of a lake. A girl appears brandishing a small bright sword. A blade appears instantly in the dreamer's hand. They fight, suddenly eye to eye, their knife hands free. Simultaneously they plunge their daggers into each other's bellies. The snake appears and rears, sinking its fangs deep into her arm. Long seconds pass, neither girl feels any pain.

Consciousness returns, and, of course, she is pregnant once again. Three weeks before the birth of her child, her grandfather dies.

The third time is after her sister returns. She has been travelling in the Far East and comes back with unwanted luggage; she doesn't know what continent the baby's father is on. There is much sorrow on the day of her sister's termination. The woman starts to bleed spontaneously. She does not bleed for nine months to follow and receives a second child. (Her sister, however, takes her husband in return.) She feels like a catcher of souls.

The fourth she loses after only one day, though she still feels the spirit pass, dragging her consciousness briefly with it towards death. A soul has been summoned and dismissed. But the spark has been lit and now it has wings for someone else.

## Keywords
ENDING, AND THE PARADOX OF CONTINUITY – DISINTEGRATION AND REUNIFICATION – LIBERATION – TRANSFORMATION – INITIATION – REJECTION OF FEAR

## Divinatory meaning
Most people at first fear this card, believing that it means physical death; but very rarely does it indicate the death of a person. It is much more likely to indicate a liberating situation in which you face, and overcome, your subconscious fear of death or fear of ending a phase in your life. This may mean admitting to insolvency, ending a bad relationship, changing a job or moving home.

## Advice
Death is transformation out of a seemingly devastating change. The whole world changes around you, and you can never be the same. There is a total change in your life; the present disintegrates and resolves itself into your future. Examine the foundations of your fears and losses. All fear is an illusion.

## Question
Are you brave enough to recognise your fears? Are you courageous enough to embrace change?

# Concept of the card

The Death card signifies death of beliefs, spiritual death and rebirth. It is on the path on which the personality learns to turn away from the life-force of desire and becomes dissolved, through spiritual death, into the higher levels of the soul at Tipareth. This is one of the three paths of initiations from the level of the personality to the true individuality. All three of these paths are traditionally seen as being paths of 'the dark night of the soul'. The other cards related to this initiation are Art and the Devil.

In the Death card of this deck the artist has layered swirling colours of energy and form over a hidden skeletal figure. Like the skull beneath the skin, death lies beneath matter and energy. As the colours come closer to the centre of the card, they dissolve into the darkness of oblivion. It is this oblivion the ego fears, unable to conceive of not existing.

But Death is a freeing of the soul so that it can evolve. The hidden skeleton holds a ring and a snake in his hands. The ring symbolises eternity, as does the *oubouros*, the snake eating its tail. In many children's tales rings are used to enter other worlds.

Death is the card of process and change; it is the death of fears and constricting belief systems. We all die many times in one lifetime, and these changes are a way of learning to accept the inevitability of physical death. Each change teaches us that we have within ourselves the ability to accept our life and our death with open arms, to embrace it and to transform ourselves. Sometimes this is unwanted and painful, but life still goes on and we can be happy again if we look beyond the present.

In alchemy, Death is represented by the process called putrefaction, the decaying black mass in the crucible which eventually turns into gold. The Death card shows us that in the depth of the blackest oblivion, lie two squares of gold. These are the seeds of the higher plane, the golden light of Tipareth into which the individual is reborn.

Initiation is an acceptance of a major change in one's life, and many initiation rituals contain a form of death. Haitian initiation ceremonies go as far as stripping the initiate's body, cleaning and purifying it and then binding it up tightly into a winding sheet. Sometimes the body is even put into the earth or a coffin.

The idea of experiencing one's own death is a very powerful one. It is transforming and similar to the idea of baptism where you are reborn from maternal waters into a new life, especially in the case of total immersion. But where Death is a freeing of the flesh, baptism is an enchaining of the soul in flesh. The closest card to this portrayal of baptism is the Devil, for he represents the enchaining of the soul in the material world. Thus Death is linked with the Devil.

The esoteric title of the Death card is the Child of the Great Transformers. This is because mankind is the child of birth and death. Old age and death are natural processes, and each generation has its chance to change the world, passing on its knowledge to the next generation. Death is part of that process of continual renewal.

The astrological sign of Scorpio is asociated with this card. Scorpio has this transforming ability and can be depicted as either a scorpion, a snake or an eagle. All three are animals linked with death: the scorpion stings itself to death when trapped; the snake sheds its skin and is a symbol of immortality; the eagle is a symbol of the soul after death. When Roman emperors were cremated, an eagle was released as a symbol of the soul ascending to the pantheon of the gods.

# Symbols associated with the card

✡ **Hebrew Letter:** *Nun* נ

✡ **Meaning:** Fish

✡ **Yetziratic Text:** Imaginative Intelligence (Change and Initiation)

✡ **Esoteric Title:** The Child of the Great Transformers

✡ **Astrology:** Scorpio ♏

✡ **Location in the Cube:** North below

✡ **Sound:** G natural

✡ **Colour:** Green-blue

✡ **Path on the Tree of Life:**
   24th – Netzach to Tipareth

# Art – 14

He clasps the stone in his hands. It has cleaved cleanly from his chest. It shines so brightly that he stands and stares into its heart, unmoving, unblinking for endless hours. The pictures begin to unfold, the mud coming to life, the molecules becoming fish, becoming birds, monkeys and men. Again and again he sees the lights, the time lines, weaving like Celtic knots. He sees the runic codes, the scriptures, the numbers and the DNA. He witnesses the process as the crystal turns to solid gold. He smiles and disappears into a billion pieces of light.

## Keywords
THE MARRIAGE OF ART, SCIENCE AND RELIGION – UNITY – A CHANNEL FOR THE DIVINE – BLENDING

## Divinatory meaning
This card represents the desire to evolve, to understand and to grow spiritually. As such, it appears in a reading when you have made a sudden leap of understanding in your life. It indicates that your creative powers are bubbling up and blending, producing external and internal harmony in your life.

## Advice

This card often turns up between two cards which may appear to relate to two different areas of your life. You may find, for instance, the Ace of Cups on one side and the Page of Wands on the other side – the beginning of a relationship and beginning of a project. When this happens it can symbolise a commixture of the two situations. This can lead you to a new understanding of how separate sides of your life relate together, allowing you to grow personally from the experience.

## Question

This is a special time: are you able to open yourself to inner harmony to find the light within?

# Concept of the card

The figure on the card of Art is the searcher. He has found his goal and is holding on to and meditating upon the golden light of Tipareth, which is also the gold of the philosopher's stone depicted in Death. Around him are the elements of earth, air, fire and water, which are mixed to create the stone. Their layering creates a rainbow effect behind the figure, similar to the rainbow bridge which you cross in meditation to reach Tipareth. The body of the searcher has almost disappeared, signifying the dissolving of his personality in the process of searching for his goal. The posture of his body indicates that his search has been directed inwards.

This path of Art goes from Yesod, at the level of the personality, to Tipareth at the level of the individuality. It moves from the astral levels of the moon to the solar levels of the Messiah centre. It is another path of 'the dark night of the soul' and represents the route mystics take to reach enlightenment.

On another level the card of Art depicts the intermingling of science, art and magic. Science is based on the principle of careful observation of nature, often by making images of it at different levels of magnification so as to see things anew. All of these images – from those produced by scanning electron microscopes to computer-enhanced pictures of star clusters – are as beautiful as any works of art. They reveal the different magical realities which exist alongside our own; another name for this card is Truth.

The Art card depicts the process of physical and spiritual evolution. The mystic has to learn to combine within him or herself the elements of earth, fire, water and air to reach divine ecstasy. Water is consciousness, which is acted upon by the spiritual force of fire, which in turn creates the airy astral imagery of meditation, which is controlled by remaining anchored in the material world of the earth. Thus, meditation is the mystic's personal alchemy for reaching the philosopher's stone.

But be warned: in combining these elements, the energy given off, like the energy created in chemical reactions, can be conducted through and into its container. Those who travel this path, both in ritual and in meditation, can become angry or can anger people around them, or both. I have seen this happen many times. This anger breaks apart old restrictions in order to allow for new growth. Truth is not an innocuous, light or trite thing – it is dangerous. Searching for the truth often produces angry young men and women and angers society in general.

Physical evolution is represented in this card in the silver circles beneath the searcher. These circles contain hidden images of an egg, a fish, a bird and a monkey. These represent the stages of evolution which have been passed through to create man as well as the stages of growth through which a human embryo goes before it looks like a child.

The astrological sign associated with this card is Sagittarius, who is represented as a centaur archer aiming his arrow high into the heavens. The centaur is half-man, half-horse. His lower half is animal, whilst his upper half is man. He aims to project himself into the heavens, thus depicting pictorially both physical and spiritual evolution.

# Symbols associated with the card

✡ **Hebrew Letter:** *Samekh* ס

✡ **Meaning:** Prop

✡ **Yetziratic Text:** The Intelligence of Probation
(The Testing)

✡ **Esoteric Titles:** The Daughter of the Reconcilers
– The Bringer Forth of Life

✡ **Astrology:** Sagittarius ♐

✡ **Location in the Cube:** West above

✡ **Sound:** G sharp

✡ **Colour:** Blue

✡ **Path on the Tree of Life:**
25th – Yesod to Tipareth

# The Devil – 15

He wants some love, so he smiles across the table, disarming in the soft light. 'More wine? So tell me more about your work, it sounds fascinating.' He draws nearer.

'Cast out? The terminology reeks of aggression and isolation – all emotions close to the Devil's heart.' He laughs. 'No need to love the Devil; but equally, no need to fear him. Negative thoughts feed fear. Destructive emotions like jealousy and rage spring from being frightened.'

He sits back in his seat to catch the waiter's eye for the bill. 'Energies must be channelled. Irrespective of gender, fears must be faced.' His head drops almost shyly, his hands drop into his lap, feigning fatigue.

'Where shall we go? Can I take you dancing? Oh! I have this book at home which you must read.' His voice trails off into the night air.

No contest. How can I resist?

## Keywords
SCAPEGOAT – LAUGHTER – SEXUALITY –
ALLOWING YOURSELF TO BE ENSLAVED BY EMPTY
DESIRES – MASCULINE ENERGY – TEMPTATION –
CREATIVITY – PROCREATIVITY

### Divinatory meaning

This card indicates a situation in which you are chained to old patterns of behaviour or in which you are a slave to your own desires. As such, it can indicate a passionate love affair in which lust triumphs over sense. Or it can indicate ambition driven by materialistic goals instead of vocation or ideals. When this card appears related to people around the questioner, it can mean being scapegoated or demonised by other people. If this is the case, beware of believing them and thus becoming more like their image of you. Use the Devil's weapon and laugh at their silly ideas, then break out and be yourself.

### Advice

Turn from materialistic temptations. Use these visions of splendour and the energy of desire to fulfil your being.

### Question

What are your desires? Are you in control of them, or are they in control of you?

# Concept of the card

The Devil conjures up all sorts of images in the minds of those brought up in a Christian culture. The most common takes the form of a man-goat, and one of the sources of this image explains perfectly the role the Devil plays in society. The Hebrews would symbolically heap all their sins on to a goat, which they then sent out into the wilderness as their scapegoat to appease God. Thus, the Devil is the embodiment of everyone's fears about themselves. Calling these emotions and passions evil, we create the Devil to embody them. Another example of such demonisation of another for one's own sins is when King Solomon looked at the polished stone floor as the Queen of Sheba was passing and said that he saw a cleft foot, when what he was referring to was her genitalia.

This path of the Devil travels from the level of the personality at Hod, earthly splendour, to the path leading to the higher levels of the soul and the individuality at Tipareth, the Messiah centre. It is the last of the paths of the 'dark night of the soul', the path of the magician and one of raw power.

In this card the Devil is part of the golden light of Tipareth, which radiates downwards from the cosmos, deep into the centre of the earth, joining mankind and the heavens. At the top of the light is an emerald eye, representing the power of the Devil, the all-seeing eye. The Devil is part of God's creation and the role he has been given is to test us. He uses our perception of the world to create illusions and tempt us. Even Christ was tested with a vision of the splendour of the material world. The Devil sends us visions of spiritual reality and spiritual illusion; by distorting reality he allows us to look at what we most fear so that we may conquer it.

Capricorn is astrologically linked with this card, and its image of a goat with a fish's tail perfectly describes the Devil's dual nature. He appears as the evil goat, but behind this illusion he is the redeeming figure of Christ represented by the fish. This is mirrored in the seemingly lustful act of sex, behind which is the redeeming function of procreation and parenthood.

Behind the two veils of colour on either side of the shaft of light are the runic shapes of magpies. Like Capricorn, the magpie is at once black and white, light and dark. The magpie is also a redeemer. These shapes represent Odin's magpie, Furze the healer. Furze sent joy into the heart with his chattering laughing call.

The Devil of black magicians is created from the group's collective bogeyman. The more terrifying they make him, the stronger they feel; whereas in reality, the less control they have over their own fears. Confronting and accepting one's fears is much more terrifying and harder to do.

The Devil gives us the power to fight our own monsters; he gives us the gift of mirth. Once we can see his ugly and monstrous distortions as comic, silly and foolish, we can laugh at ourselves and our fears, and we can rise higher up the Tree of Life. Paul Case cites a hymn to the sun-god Ra to encapsulate the initiation of this path: 'Thy priests go forth and greet the dawn and wash their hearts with laughter.'

Once we can learn to laugh at ourselves, the Devil changes from being the sterile monster of our nightmares into Pan, in his aspect as the creative, passionate, mischievous symbol of sexuality and the god of Spring. Pan's energies are masculine, sexual and creative. Sexual energy is the desire and the drive to procreate in order to continue the race. These energies can also be directed from physical evolution to the spiritual evolution of the soul in our inner spiritual life. Our Western culture has taught us that the body and spirit are separate, but saints and priests refrain from sex in order to direct these energies elsewhere.

## Symbols associated with the card

✿ **Hebrew Letter:** *Ayin* ע

✿ **Meaning:** Eye

✿ **Yetziratic Text:** Renovating Intelligence (Laughter)

✿ **Esoteric Titles:** The Lord of the Gates of Matter –
The Child of the Forces of Time

✿ **Astrology:** Capricorn ♑

✿ **Location in the Cube:** West below

✿ **Sound:** A natural

✿ **Colour:** Indigo

✿ **Path on the Tree of Life:**
26th – Hod to Tipareth

# The Tower – 16

There is a worm in his belly, he ate it whilst he was still a child. It has grown with him into adulthood and lies in his gut, turgid, secreting a mixture of strange substances – some soothing, some noxious, but very many with hallucinogenic properties.

By his early twenties his behaviour is increasingly led by the worm's fluid. He meets a woman and they have a son. The child finds echoes within his father's soul. 'How like me he is,' the father thinks. But the child is without a worm and grows closer to the mother. Mother and son's dreams and hopes are not fed by the parasite, so the reality in which they live is very different.

On the morning of the child's eighth birthday the worm creates a particularly bitter putrefaction, manifesting cruelly within the host. The little boy takes his father's hands, 'Why do you keep a worm in your belly that makes you hurt so?'

But the toxins are strong in the father and he strikes the child, drawing blood.

The next morning his family is gone. He is left alone in his castle. He rattles around it day after day, cursing and humming in an unhappy insanity.

He shuts himself in the east tower, resolved to starve

out the worm. For thirty days he eats and drinks nothing, but still he thrives. The worm feeds him, keeping him alive, refusing to let his host die. It is feeding on his fears and misery, and sustaining him in return.

Years pass and the tower grows dark and rickety, the man is ageing slowly, but the fire burning in his eyes never wanes. In his sleep there is no escape, his dreams are filled with writhing serpents in combat, feeding, copulating, ever increasing in their numbers.

One dusk, a stranger unexpectedly arrives. It is his son. For a moment love and hope floods through, silencing the worm temporarily. With great tenderness the son takes his father's hands again. 'Release the worm,' he whispers and begins to sing.

Slowly, his father's expression begins to alter. It betrays every emotion in sequence, until his entire being is engulfed with rage, pain and torment. Shuddering and weeping he too begins to sing.

The release is inevitable, the stench of the past unmistakable in the father's mouth as he belches up vileness. It coils and flexes in the turret around them. Hand in hand, they run, still singing. Above them the heavens open, cleansing them as they enter the gardens. They turn to stare as lightning crashes and splatters out of the heavens. It shatters the pinnacles and the staircases, splitting the stone, finally burying the Snake of Despite he had cradled within. From that day on, he has slept the dreamless sleep of a soul at peace.

## Keywords
HEALING PROCESS – DEMOLITION OF THE EGO – LEARNING – INTENSE EMOTIONAL CHANGES – GROWTH

## Divinatory meaning
You have been holding on to a particular perception of reality which no longer fits. You have been clinging on to this so much that you have become afraid to look at the world as it really is. You have been afraid to face up to the changes happening all around you. Suddenly this mental Tower is shattered and reality comes flooding in.

## Advice
The Tower describes an emotional trauma, which will vary in intensity depending on how long you have been holding out against accepting your new self. Aleister Crowley uses the analogy of the intense, but brief, pain of

tooth extraction, which ultimately brings long-term relief. The trauma is the cure, not the illness. Allow this to happen. Embrace the pain and prepare the ground for self-knowledge and healing. The more you cling on to your old perceptions of reality, the harder it will be to break them, and their inevitable collapse will be more painful.

### Question
Are you prepared to accept the loss of your old beliefs? What have you got to lose?

# Concept of the card

The Tower on this card represents the personality. It is built like a body, with a ball-like finial for the head, twin turrets reaching out like arms, a waisted support in the middle and a portal dividing the tower like legs at the bottom. We build our personality like this Tower; the personality is not the whole of ourselves, but is instead the mask behind which our souls exist.

The Tower is being shattered by a force from above in the way that the personality is shattered by the light of understanding sent down by the higher self. This force transmutes the matter of our ego and turns it from solid into fluid; as water rushes down the sides of the Tower, so our emotions break out under stress.

The Hebrew letter for the card means mouth, representing the destructive power of communication and sound. Joshua destroyed the walls of Jericho with the noise of trumpets. Our own ego can be destroyed by the words uttered from people's mouths as well as by whispers of our inner voice.

The Tower also represents all constructed institutions, be they political, economic or religious. When institutions become too attached to outdated ideas, they too can be destroyed through the power of the word. They can also be saved by words, and this is the magic of the spin doctor for he can build or destroy with voice alone.

The path of the Tower lies between reason and emotion, between Hod and Netzach. This is the balancing path of the personality and ego. The Tower has similarities to the Death card, but instead of representing rebirth and completion, it describes trauma and healing.

Mars is the planet associated with the path because it is closely connected with war. War has the power to pull down and destroy whole cultures; but with war comes sudden scientific insight and massive cultural change by which both the victor and the defeated are affected. After the Second World War, Britain found itself irreversibly changed, both socially and within the power structure of the world. Germany and Japan were able to rise like phoenixes from the ashes of their defeat.

The story of the Tower of Babel contains within it the seeds of all these ideas. After the flood, the descendants of Noah settled in Babylonia to build a city of brick. They decided to build a Tower, in an attempt to conquer heaven. God struck the Tower down with a bolt of lightning and, as punishment, imposed different languages on them. Where before they had been able to communicate and work in union, now they could not understand one another. Thus, they could never again come together to threaten the heavens. Their languages caused misunderstandings and sowed the seeds of cultural and racial mistrust.

The Tower is the myth of the creation of race, mirroring the idea that we are all closely related genetically, divided by our cultures rather than our bodies. Cultures are social masks of personality. Once they can be shattered by the quiet voice of peace, we may once again be able to reach out in unison and truly conquer the heavens.

# Symbols associated with the card

✡ **Hebrew Letter:** *Peh* פ

✡ **Meaning:** Mouth

✡ **Yetziratic Text:** Active Intelligence (The Disintegrating Ego)

✡ **Esoteric Title:** The Lord of the Host of the Mighty

✡ **Astrology:** Mars ♂

✡ **Location in the Cube:** North

✡ **Sound:** C natural

✡ **Colour:** Scarlet

✡ **Path on the Tree of Life:**
27th – Hod to Netzach

# The Star – 17

She lives in a large, rambling house, set back from the river. The ford is upstream from her moorings. When travellers cross, their sorrows, hopes and dreams are washed out and carried downstream into the welcoming embrace of her nets. Every morning she quietly collects these gossamer desires and hopes, taking them back to her workshop. From these she spends hours and years forging and sculpting figurines, animals, votive offerings, fetishes and charms. She wraps these in tiny prayers, selling them for ha'penny bits, which have long since ceased to be currency.

## Keywords
**HOPE – SPIRITUALITY – INSPIRATION – HEALING – CLARITY OF MOTIVATION – PEACE – CREATIVITY**

## Divinatory meaning
This card brings hope and peaceful joy into your life. Whereas Lust represents driven and manic inspiration, the Star is sweet and gentle inspiration from the Muse. It brings about a realisation of peace and beauty in your life, and a quiet acceptance of happiness and success. It heralds a gradual drifting up to new levels of consciousness.

## Advice

This card often appears after a period of emotional upheaval, and as such it heralds the end of turmoil. The Star gives you the space to find the peace you need for inner healing. When this card appears, you will be blessed with sweet hope – drink your fill. This time is a healing time, let the balsam pour freely.

## Question

What parts of your life most need rejuvenating?

# Concept of the card

The Star shines above a woman whose hair curls out like antennae, collecting the energies at this level and directing them through her hands in an everlasting flow to earth. The Star is astrologically associated with Aquarius, the water-bearer who pours out his gifts to earth. The Star is the manifestation of beauty from the goddess, and her breasts feed us with inspiration; she is the beauty which inspired Pygmalion to create life.

Around the woman are the four colours of the North American Indian elements. East is yellow-orange and associated with fire; south is red and associated with the life-blood and water; the west is blue-black and associated with earth; north is white and associated with air. The universe is resolved into the elements, which she pours freely from her hands, assured that the energy of the heavens will keep her continually supplied.

The Star is the energy of imagination and the inspiration of the Muses; it is the highest level of human emotion. The Star is a vision of Eden and the world perfected; it is a sunny day in the countryside, an invigorating walk by a stormy sea, the serenity and clarity of mountain air and the warm hypnosis of the flickering flames of an open fire.

The path of the Star runs from Netzach, who is beauty, creativity, emotion and victory, to Yesod, the foundation and the astral levels. It is the vision of the beauty of nature that inspires the personality.

The Hebrew letter for the Star, *tzaddi*, is the fish hook of meditation which catches our dreams and visions. It the calm voice pouring balm on to the spirit; it is the sense of quiet hope.

# Symbols associated with the card

✡ **Hebrew Letter:** *Tzaddi* צ

✡ **Meaning:** Fish hook

✡ **Yetziratic Text:** Natural Intelligence (The Peace of the Universe)

✡ **Esoteric Titles:** The Daughter of the Firmament – The Dweller Between the Waters

✡ **Astrology:** Aquarius ♒

✡ **Location in the Cube:** South above

✡ **Sound:** A sharp

✡ **Colour:** Violet

✡ **Path on the Tree of Life:**
Netzach to Yesod

# The Moon – 18

The Fool lies staring into the ripples he crossed earlier that year. His companions have travelled on without him, but the Fool has remained. Uncertain of direction, resting under the willows, eyes lulled by the flickering moonlight, he hardly notices the woman crouching beside him. She smiles and presses a flask and a small key into his hands. He smiles up at her, but she has gone.

Propping himself up on his elbows, he uncorks the bottle and inhales deeply. Although he does not recognise or trust the odour, he drinks long and deeply of the amber-red liquid.

The next morning there is no trace of the Fool, save a brightly bedecked tricorn hat, with bells and feathers jangling in the nets of the dream-fisher.

## Keywords
INITIATION – CHALLENGE – DREAMS – DECEPTION – FEMININE SEXUALITY – ILLUSIONS – PARANOIA

### Divinatory meaning

The Moon indicates a time when you are bombarded by conflicting opinions and evidence as to what to do for the best. Unfortunately, this is also a time when you cannot trust your own ability to see things rationally. What you think you can see clearly is just a reflection; it is all the wrong way round and the true colours do not show. The solution to your problems is more likely to appear in dreams and visions than through rational thought.

This card can also bring paranoia and fears to the surface. They may have little or no foundations, being merely the result of past problems and low self-esteem.

### Advice

Meditation on the inner light can be a calming influence at this time. When you look in the mirror of the moon she reflects back the things you hide from yourself, magnifying them in the process. Do not be afraid to experience these new ways of seeing yourself and your situation. Examine all your options. You alone are responsible for yourself and your emotions. Do nothing out of mere curiosity.

### Question

What are your fears around this situation? List them. What is the worst that can actually happen? How likely is it actually to happen?

# Concept of the card

On the Tree of Life the watery path of the Moon travels from the earth at Malkulth to the feminine powers of emotion and victory at Netzach. This is the path of the creative inspiration of artist and poets, whereas the Aeon is the inspiration of the rational and the scientific minds.

The Moon is a mirror to the Sun, or Tipareth, which is the light from the higher levels. The Moon reflects this light on her light side, although she always has one hidden and shadowy side. She distorts the images from the higher levels and has none of the warmth associated with directly radiated light. Thus, her images are hardly coloured and faint, like phantoms.

Tradition says that treading the path of the Moon successfully confirms an ability in 'bewitchment and casting illusions'. When we understand the visions of our dreams we can understand those of others; we can then manipulate these qualities in ourselves and others. It is on this path that psychologists trace our inner personality and the ways it is changed by experience. This is represented by the key-like symbol beside the Moon.

The Moon is also the card of night for it represents the death of day. *Qoph*, the Hebrew letter for this card, means sleep. The Moon is the ruler of our sleep, and she appears on the card as if glimmering palely in our dreams, creating the watery pools of imagination from which the shining oily monsters of madness or lunacy slither. Where the Sun relaxes us and makes us happy, the Moon makes us tremble and nervous with unexplained anticipation.

The Hebrew letter *qoph* also means the back of the head, and this is the part of the body the Moon controls. She has power over the cerebellum and the medulla oblongata; they connect with the limbic system which guards occult powers. These also regulate the areas of the body maintaining life-sustaining body functions during sleep. They are vital, vulnerable and invisible.

The Moon in this card has a halo around it. This halo is shaped like a fish, the sign of Pisces and the dreamers of the zodiac. The halo represents the gravitational pull the Moon exerts on the tides of the earth. Its shape resembles a vagina, reminding us of the power the Moon has over the menstrual tides of the female body. It is at these times that the Moon has women in her power and the periods when women are most psychic.

# Symbols associated with the card

✡ **Hebrew Letter:** *Qoph* ק

✡ **Meaning:** Sleep, back of the head

✡ **Yetziratic Text:** Corporeal Intelligence (Illusions)

✡ **Esoteric Titles:** The Rulers of Flux and Reflux – The Child of the Sons of the Mighty

✡ **Astrology:** Pisces ♓

✡ **Location in the Cube:** South below

✡ **Sound:** B natural

✡ **Colours:** Crimson – Ultraviolet

✡ **Path on the Tree of Life:**
29th – Malkulth to Netzach

# The Sun – 19

The children are betrothed at birth. Now they travel to the lands of the bride's uncle to be married, their journey guided by a scholar monk, a Fool. Huge amounts of property are at stake.

They travel for twelve years, circling the earth. They come to a crossroads with a ford – they cannot continue the plans of their parents. So each sets off to find their own destiny – one north and one south. Each turns their back and walks until they forget.

So many adventures and challenges present themselves that each grows strong and contented. Still, they walk around the world until they arrive back at the crossing. Instantly they recognise one another and laugh, delighted. Linking arms, they head west once more in silent joy.

## Keywords
DIVINITY – MIRACLES – LOVE – TRUTH – JOY –
HAPPINESS – SUCCESS

## Divinatory meaning
This is a time of optimism and pure bliss; the warmth of
joy radiates upon you and from you. It is a time when
your inner child comes to the fore, and barriers within
you and between other people melt. Current partnerships
go well, and love is freely given and received.

## Advice
One of the most precious gifts in life is the ability to
realise just how happy you are – not just looking back
upon an event, but at the time of the event. To be able to
experience pure bliss in the moment and not just savour
nostalgia is a gift indeed.

## Question
Do you secretly feel the need to sabotage your joy? When
all is light, do you hunt desperately for the dark? When
you find yourself wailing in the dark, visualise yourself
filled with light.

# Concept of the card

The Sun on this card shines above a walled garden. It is Eden, the earthly
paradise or secret garden of our childhood, the place where we played and
learned to be ourselves. Thus, the Sun represents the time of freedom and
innocence just before adolescence, when male and female can innocently
coexist. It is the point of childhood when our emerging personality breaks
free and flowers, ready to be tested by the first storms of adolescence.

Below the garden are two heads, representing the masculine and the
feminine. Their faces are masked by the joyous child within them, the
purest form of their personality. At the bottom, their hands join to form the
roots which hold the Tree of Life. Beyond the tree is a golden path, the
road on which we can return to the higher self, if we learn how through
meditation on the Tree of Life.

The Sun also controls the seasons of the year. The seasonal rituals our
ancestors incorporated into their religions remind us of the Sun's
importance to them as the maintainer of life on earth. They feared that the
Sun would not return if not worshipped properly or sacrificed to regularly.
Without the Sun there is no harvest, and with too much Sun there is
drought. Even in the so-called First World, where we like to forget our debt
to nature, the Sun causes damage to our skins and its flares interrupt and
damage our communication systems.

The Sun is the creator of the personality. On the Tree of Life it is the path where the intellectual level of the personality, in Hod, is affected by the astral levels in Yesod. The joining of both creates the form of the personality, or the mask we wear on earth. It is this mask which is described in an astrological birth chart. This path is the highest level of the human intellect, whereas the Star is the highest level of human emotions. The Hebrew word *resh* means head, which is consistent with the idea that this is the path of the intellect acted upon by the astral levels. When travelling this path we can meet the other personalities which we have held during other incarnations.

The Sun is called the Collecting Intelligence, and in alchemy it represents the crucible, the collecting vehicle of the spirit. It is where the higher self functions through the personality as it is brought to the lower planes, in the same way that the pure spirit reaches to the higher self at the levels above.

## Symbols associated with the card

- **Hebrew Letter:** *Resh* ר
- **Meaning:** Head
- **Yetziratic Text:** Collecting Intelligence (The Personality)
- **Esoteric Title:** The Lord of the Fire of the World
- **Astrology:** Sun ☉
- **Location in the Cube:** South
- **Sound:** D natural
- **Colour:** Orange
- **Path on the Tree of Life:** 30th – Yesod to Hod

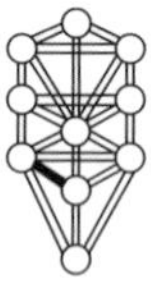

# The Aeon – 20

The Fool floats downstream with the keys clasped firmly in his hands, face upwards, smiling as the dark cool waters carry him. The waters become the Cosmos, which in turn he feels expanding infinitely within the confines of his mouth. He sees everything, feels everything. He is the smallest electron and the largest star, a tiny speck of light travelling at a constant speed on an eternally spiralling time line, emitting satellite 'lives' as it moves steadily along its trajectory. The Fool experiences many journeys, many lives, many souls. When he is ready, he arrives at a single luminous door.

## Keywords
MACRO AND MICRO – ULTIMATE PARADOX – OBJECTIVE – ABSOLUTE COMPREHENSION – TOTALLY INTEGRATED – FULLY CONSCIOUS

## Divinatory meaning
The Aeon signifies a recognition that externally things are about to change, that internally you have already changed and that you have been tested. Its presence in a reading brings about a karmic understanding of the

situation you are in, along with an evaluation of one's efforts and accomplishments from a higher plane.

### Advice

This card brings about a new understanding of how you fit into the universe and what that universe is. Beware of becoming too judgemental of others, of pointing out the sins of others whilst missing those very same sins in yourself. Remember, the wise man knows he is a fool and the fool thinks he is wise.

### Question

How does this new understanding change your goals and aims?

## Concept of the card

The change in the title of this card from Judgement to Aeon was made by Aleister Crowley. He believed the idea of a last judgement belonged to the passing Age of Pisces and he wanted to take the opportunity to represent his idea of the essence of the next Aeon through this card.

The new Aeon is upon us, dissolving old forms of religion and thought. It represents the cool fire of desire, which burns away the material and raises up the soul. The new Aeon is the mingling of art, magic and science; it can be seen in the beauty of fractals and the poetry of quantum physics. The image on the Aeon card is of atoms, quarks and gluons, of galaxies and of cells; it is an image of our planet from space and of the inner eye with which we see it all, the dream-time. The Aeon is the fearful symmetry.

The path on the Tree of Life associated with the Aeon joins the material at the level of Malkulth, with the idea of splendour, at the level of Hod. This path is the beauty of nature and science. In this card we see the material from a higher plane for it is the intellectual path on the astral level, rather than the emotional path of the Moon.

The element associated with this card is fire. The Aeon represents the fiery inspiration and leap of understanding that allows us to see the true splendour of the physical world. The discovery of the ability to create and control fire was itself one of the most important leaps made by humanity. It assisted us in controlling our environment, allowed us to cook our food, to mould and intermingle metals and to burn fuels to release the enormous amount of energy needed to take us out of the orbit of earth and into space.

The symbol for the Hebrew word associated with the Aeon, *shin*, looks like the flames of the fire; but the Hebrew meaning is tooth. Thus, the Aeon is the testing ground of theories, in the same way that jewellers would bite a gold coin to test its softness and check that it was real.

Pluto is the planet associated with this path. Pluto is associated with material wealth, an analytical frame of mind, big business and hidden power. But coupled with the Age of Aquarius, we see that the next Aeon has tendencies to global humanitarian preoccupations, balanced equally by hidden global business networks and global communications. All these elements will form the new consciousness, as will great leaps of discovery and understanding in the field of science. These will help us to understand our links to the universe beyond the globe and will change our perceptions of reality.

# Symbols associated with the card

✡ **Hebrew Letter:** *Shin* שׁ

✡ **Meaning:** Tooth

✡ **Yetziratic Text:** The Perpetual Intelligence (The Discoveries of Science)

✡ **Esoteric Title:** The Spirit of Primal Fire

✡ **Element:** Fire △

A **Astrology:** Pluto ♇

✡ **Location in the Cube:** North to south

✡ **Sound:** C natural

✡ **Colour:** Glowing orange scarlet

✡ **Path on the Tree of Life:**
31st – Malkulth to Hod

# The Universe – 21

The Fool leaps into a river and is borne by the current, past a child playing dominoes, past a swan. He rests at the house of a woman of many colours and many children. Two befriend him and follow him as he walks on through the lands of a wise knight.

There he is taught by a master and becomes a priest-clown. He and the children travel north with the gypsies to the City of Souls, where he learns the science of spirit. He is offered tutorage in the city's delights. They travel through the great abyss, through famine and war, through ruined towers and fortresses. When they come to a ford, the children are almost adult, and so they part ways.

The Fool sits at the crossing until he is given the gift of a key. He steps through the door, turning inside out, seeing all and nothing, becoming star light and resting – until a microsecond later he is once more opening a door, once again running down a hill side and leaping anew into the river.

streams of love flow and flow
and ever inwards grow and grow
towards my soul to it entwine
to end my sorrows to end all time
to sleep and dream
whilst still with love
to swim in thought and rest with life

## Keywords
COMPLETION – LIBERATION – I AND I – DIVINE LIFE –
DEATH OF THE EGO – REBIRTH OF THE PURE SOUL –
DIVINE LIGHT

## Divinatory meaning
Whatever area of your life this card relates to, it signifies
a gaining of goals, bringing satisfaction, completion and
success. As well as indicating success, this can also be an
interlude where one simply exists, when being is more
important than doing. This is very difficult to do or
understand when you are younger, but as you grow older
there is a realisation that simply existing, being at one
with yourself and the universe, is the essence of life.

## Advice
Success can be frightening, especially if your ego is
bound up with a desire for personal attainment. Once you
have achieved your goals, your personality wonders what
there is left to do. It thus faces a small death. Therefore,
the true gift of success is not seeing yourself in the mirror
as a brilliant, beautiful and successful person, but the
realisation that you can step off your own personal
merry-go-round. You can cease striving for a perfect life
and instead find peace, and just be.

## Question
You have finished one stage of your life, with one door
shutting behind you. What is behind the closed door?
Turn round and look at the next door opening. What do
you see?

# Concept of the card

Is the illustration on this card the vastness of space, where great clouds of
coloured gasses form and shape into planets and stars or is it the view from
within an atom, of the alchemy of forces and particles which create matter?
All are one and the same. This is the magic of which the great wizards
spoke. It is the doorway to understanding the creation of the Universe, and
the matter and meaning from which all the other cards emanate.

The Universe is the doorway to the astral levels as seen in the eye of the mind; it is the centre door through the mandala of meditation; it is stepping out of one perception and into another.

The Universe is on the path where Malkulth, the earth, joins with Yesod, the foundation of the astral levels. The astral levels are realms of magical and illusory fantasies, of visions of the higher levels, and nightmares created from fears and trapped energies in our own psyches. The path this card is on is called The Great One of the Night Time because most people only reach these astral levels in their dreams. Day-dreaming and conscious meditation are a more controlled form of travelling this path.

As you travel upwards on the Tree of Life the Universe is the first path and the Fool the last. In the same way, the Hebrew letter *tau* is the last letter of the Hebrew alphabet. Between *aleph*, the first letter of the alphabet representing the Fool, and *tau*, the letter for the Universe, the Tree describes the whole of creation, the alpha and omega.

*Tau* means cross and its position on the Cube of Space is directly in the centre – the cross is a means of marking the centre. From the cross of Christ to the Indian swastika, it is a common symbol of redemption.

The lesson of the Universe card is taught by its ruling planet, Saturn. In astrological terms Saturn is the taskmaster; he sets the great tests during our lifetimes, he is karma. Saturn is also a teacher and with these tests he helps us to move upwards, to evolve. He decrees that we should still be kept in bondage by matter and time on the level of Malkulth. But we have been given the gift of meditation, which allows us to contact our higher selves and receive wisdom and understanding to help us pass the tests – if we have ears to hear and eyes to see. The Tarot cards themselves are part of this assistance to mankind.

# Symbols associated with the card

✡ **Hebrew Letter:** *Tau* ת

✡ **Meaning:** Equal armed cross

✡ **Yetziratic Text:** The Administrative Intelligence (The Laws of Nature)

✡ **Esoteric Title**: The Great One of the Night Time

✡ **Astrology:** Saturn ♄

✡ **Location in the Cube:** Centre

✡ **Sound:** A natural

✡ **Colour:** Indigo

✡ **Path on the Tree of Life:** 32nd – Malkulth to Yesod

# THE FOUR SUITS

♦

## Wands

### Keywords
THE EGO – HOW YOU RELATE TO YOURSELF

The wand is a wooden sword which burns. As the flaming sword at the gates to the garden of Eden, it illuminates and burns with the dynamic energy of Chokmah, transforming the physical and leaving behind a residue of heat, smoke and ashes.

The wand is a magical tool to bring down the energies of the universe, using them to transform the physical. It acts as a bridge from the powers above to the powers below.

In mythology wooden wands contained within them the magical possibility of life, even after having been broken from a tree. When Joseph of Arimathea struck his magical staff into the ground on Wearyall Hill in Glastonbury, the wand took root and grew, and became the mythological Holy Thorn, which blooms only at Christmas.

Of the four Grail Hallows, wands is related to the spear. This spear belonged to the Roman centurion, St Longinus, who used his spear to pierce Christ's side and quicken his death whilst on the cross, and thus quicken the redemption of humanity. This spear traditionally appears in visions to Grail seekers, dripping with Christ's blood. It is also said to have the power to heal the sick with just one stroke.

The flaming spear also dealt the dolorous wound to the Fisher King's thigh or genitals, enchaining the land and making it barren. This started the search for the Grail, or the feminine side of the male, and it could not succeed until the Grail seekers and the Fisher King realised that the king and the land were one.

In Celtic mythology the wand is the spear of Lugh, the god of the sun. Lugh is killed every year with the harvest, his death remembered in the ritual of Lamas or Lughomass. He was a warrior god whose spear was magical, thirsting for blood and flashing and roaring in battle like lightning.

In Tarot cards wands represent energy and passion on all levels – physical and sexual, intellectual and spiritual. It is an energy that forces its way through the ego, and deals directly with our emotions, drives and visions. Thus, the wands are an assessment of our core nature. In other words, wands are torches that burn through the masks of the personality and directly illuminate the true self. Wands show us the bright side of our emotional identity; they explain how we interact with and relate to others.

The fire the wand controls is the fire of the spirit, the energy of Chokmah. This was the all-consuming fire stolen by Prometheus to give to humanity. It creates sexual desire, ambition and dreams, which in turn inspire creativity. But misused or out of control, the energies wands give off magnify emotions, engendering anger and hatred. Recognise the source of your emotions, understand them, and they will lose their power over you.

# Symbols associated with the suit

✿ **Hebrew Letter:** *Yod* ’

✿ **Astrology:** Aries – Leo – Sagittarius ♈ ♌ ♐

✿ **Element:** Fire △

✿ **World:** Atziluth

✿ **Energy:** Dynamic

✿ **Sexual Energy:** Yin – male

✿ **Humour:** Choleric (extrovert, liable to anger, quick and strong)

✿ **Quadruplicity:** Spirit

✿ **Season:** Spring

✿ **Sephira on the Tree of Life:** Chokmah

# Cups

## Keywords
HOW YOU RELATE TO OTHERS –
RELATIONSHIPS

A cup represents any kind of vessel for holding other things. It can be a womb or a cauldron, the Grail or a bucket, even a washing machine! Whereas wands represent the dynamic regenerative energy of yin and maleness, cups are the formative regenerative energy of yang and femaleness. Wands energise the self by striking to the core and vibrating power through the whole, whereas cups contain, mix together and synthesise.

The cup has many associations, such as the communal wassail-bowl or loving-cup filled with intoxicating liquor and passed round for all to drink from and thus partake in the spirit of the community. The Holy Grail of the female side of the Christian mysteries is a similar vessel. It contains the blood of the Eucharist, which can be seen as the male equivalent of women's menstrual blood. It thus reveals the chalice as the womb in which Christ is reborn in all of us, as it holds his creative life-force.

Many Celtic stories tell of a cauldron that magically replenishes itself eternally. It provides nourishment for everyone, in much the same way that Demeter, the Greek goddess of fertility and nature, uses her cornucopia, or horn of plenty. Indeed, Demeter's cornucopia resembles a woman's antler-like fallopian tubes and ovaries.

The cups of the Tarot contain the food of life – that is, love, in all its forms, be it spiritual, emotional or physical. The liquid in the Tarot cups comes from the great sea of Binah on the Tree of Life; it is the fluid soul of the world, contained in the first created form. Thus, the cups are the vehicle for expressing the collective soul, whose vibrations appear to us as fleeting memories in our dreams.

The Tarot cups are containers of emotions: they mix the influences around them, reflecting them back to their source. In readings cups deal with interpersonal relationships, embodying how you relate to other people. Water runs in channels, and we all have our own philosophies, histories and cultures that define and contextualise love; but we should try to be open to the wider applications of love.

# Symbols associated with the suit

✡ **Hebrew Letter:** *Heh* הֵ

✡ **Astrology:** Cancer – Scorpio – Pisces ♋ ♏ ♓

✡ **Element:** Water ▽

✡ **World:** Briah

✡ **Energy:** Love

✡ **Sexual Energy:** Yang – female

✡ **Humour:** Phlegmatic (introverted, calm, strong but lacking in vivacity)

✡ **Quadruplicity:** Emotion

✡ **Season:** Summer

✡ **Sephira on the Tree of Life:** Binah

# Swords

## Keywords
### THE INTELLECT – CHOICES OF LOGIC

The sword in these Tarot cards is made up of a composite image representing objects that hold the same energy as the sword. A sword may be a pen, a gun, a plough or a hypodermic needle; all are used to transform the old and create anew; all dissolve and destroy physically, spiritually and emotionally; all are tools of power. How they are used is up to those who wield them; what is destroyed is their choice.

Swords represent the intellect, which divides, analyses and creates anew. The intellect's rationality has no time for sentimentality, it sees only the vision of what it wants to create as it is in the process of destroying the old. Thus, swords symbolise the way that thought can cut down and destroy old structures and ideas to bring through the new. In the same way, the intellect is used to empower or destroy individuals, groups or whole nations.

In mythology swords represent the powers of destruction and annihilation, regardless of whether those powers are used to destroy good or evil. Saint Michael, the warrior archangel, carries a sword to slay the devil. The sword Excalibur wielded by King Arthur gave him the power to annihilate his enemies. This power helped him create his kingdom from lands once ravaged by the wars of disparate nobles fighting to control each other's territories.

Swords contain the energy of Geburah, the sephira, or point on the Tree of Life, of destruction and disintegration. But this energy should not be seen as evil. Swords belong to the element of air, an energy which not only disperses old stale structures into nothingness, but which also fuels the sparks of the new life. Thus, air breathes new life into old.

Swords represent the intellectual choices we make in life. Sometimes we are presented with problems which can only be solved by breaking free of the patterns of behaviour we have learned to follow due to cultural and social pressures. These intellectual choices can force us to take particular actions that may seem drastic or hard. However, by taking these actions and making these choices, we can overcome seemingly unsolvable problems by creating a totally new situation, sweeping away our old selves in order to create ourselves anew.

The energy represented by the sword is a powerful tool, and its use carries with it moral implications. Just as the hypodermic needle can bring relief from pain and illness and create miraculous visions, it can also create pain and emotional chaos and destroy the health of the mind and body of the recipient. Always be aware that the choices you make are your own.

# Symbols associated with the suit

✡ **Hebrew Letter:** *Vau* ‏ו‎

✡ **Astrology:** Libra – Aquarius – Gemini ♎ ♒ ♊

✡ **Element:** Air △

✡ **World:** Yetzirah

✡ **Energy:** Dissolution

✡ **Sexual Energy:** Yin – male

✡ **Humour:** Sanguine (extrovert, quick, confident but changeable)

✡ **Quadruplicity:** Intellect

✡ **Season:** Autumn

✡ **Sephira on the Tree of Life:** Geburah

# Discs

## Keywords
OUR PHYSICAL BOUNDARIES –
THE MATERIAL WORLD

Discs represent the earth; they represent the material and physical world and also what we create in this world. Discs represent sovereign countries as a whole, as well as the fruits and wealth of that country such as agriculture, minerals and metals obtained from the earth. Discs also represent manufacturing and other business endeavours.

Discs symbolise the land of the king. In mythology this is represented by the stone of destiny. King Arthur pulled his sword Excalibur from such a stone; the Stone of Scone was placed under the throne on which the Kings of Scotland were crowned. This stone was seized by the English, and since James I and VI it has been used at the coronations of British monarchs. (It has since been returned to Scotland.)

Discs also represent the security and stability of the country, the home and one's possessions. They indicate the progress of our careers. Discs represent the purely physical side of attraction and sexuality as well as indicating our physical health and well-being.

The energy represented in the discs are the feminine aspects of fruitfulness and form at Binah, energised with the creative force of Chesed. He is the merciful king, the builder and architect who creates and makes the structures of the land and carries out the divine plan of God. The energy of the discs is sometimes symbolised by Arthur's round table, as this was the structure around which he created a balanced and organised society in his kingdom.

Discs represent the structures and institutions of society. They describe how these elements affect and control the individual. Thus, discs in a reading can refer to marriage, family, academic education and learning, politics, government, the power of businessmen, generals or politicians, organised religion or career. These structure and control how we individually express the formative creative energies within us, our emotions, our intellect and our spirituality.

# Symbols associated with the suit

✡ **Hebrew Letter:** *Heh* הֵ

✡ **Astrology:** Capricorn – Taurus – Virgo ♑ ♉ ♍

✡ **Element:** Earth ▽

✡ **World:** Assiah

✡ **Energy:** Structure

✡ **Sexual Energy:** Yang – female

✡ **Humour:** Melancholic (introverted, pensive and tending to sadness)

✡ **Quadruplicity:** Physical

✡ **Season:** Winter

✡ **Sephira on the Tree of Life:** Malkulth

# THE NUMBER CARDS

♦

## Aces ●

### Keywords
OWN – WONDER – ONENESS – ENTIRETY –
WHOLENESS – THE INDIVIDUAL – COMPLETENESS –
I AND I – THE WHOLE WITHIN

### Divinatory meaning
Aces signify the will to create. They herald the type of
beginning expressed by the essence of each suit. They are
more powerful in readings than the other number cards,
as they represent both the seeds of new directions in the
life of the questioner and the roots from which the cards
surrounding them draw their energy.

### Symbols associated with the number

✡ **Relation to the Suit:** The seed or root of the element

✡ **Sephira on the Tree of Life:**
   Kether and Malkulth

## Twos

### Keywords
TO SHARE – TO GIVE – TOO – ALSO – COLLECTIVE –
DIVISION – DUALITY

### Divinatory meaning
Twos are two points or energies coming together,
representing the energy of the suit in balance. Twos thus
signify love, unity and partnerships.

## Symbols associated with the number

✧ **Relation to the Suit:** Balancing the energies of the element

✧ **Sephira on the Tree of Life:** Chokmah

# Threes △

## Keywords
TRY – INTENSITY – ENERGY

## Divinatory meaning
When two energies come together a third is created. Thus, threes represent fertility, or the full expression or blossoming of the energies of each suit, both on the physical and emotional levels.

## Symbols associated with the number

✧ **Relation to the Suit:** Growth and fertility as represented by the element

✧ **Sephira on the Tree of Life:** Binah

# Fours ▢

## Keywords
FAIR – PURPOSE – COMPLEXITIES

## Divinatory meaning
Four points or energies linked together create a square. Thus, fours signify a stable structure, as expressed by the energies of each suit.

## Symbols associated with the number

✧ **Relation to the Suit:** Establishing foundations using the element

✧ **Sephira on the Tree of Life:** Chesed

# Fives

## Keywords
FIGHT – FIRE – WINNING OR LOSING – GAMES –
STRATEGIES – RULES – INTENT

## Divinatory meaning
With fives, another point or energy joins those in the
square, unbalancing what was stable. Thus, fives
represent loss and conflict, as expressed by the energies
of each suit.

## Symbols associated with the number

✡ **Relation to the Suit:** Upsetting the stability of the element

✡ **Sephira on the Tree of Life:** Geburah

# Sixes

## Keywords
CEASE – SATISFACTION – SUCCESS – ASSIMILATION –
MOTION

## Divinatory meaning
In the six, another energy joins the five, and thus stability
is regained and strengthened. Sixes represent victory and
expansion of the energies of each suit.

## Symbols associated with the number

✡ **Relation to the Suit:** Victory for the element

✡ **Sephira on the Tree of Life**: Tipareth

# Sevens ◯

### Keywords
SEVERE – ACCELERATION – MISUSE OF ENERGY –
CONFLICTS

### Divinatory meaning
In the sevens stability is again tilted off balance by the
gaining of another energy. This time there is a frantic
struggle to regain the equilibrium lost, as the other
energies fight against the new. Thus, sevens represent an
over-exertion of the energies represented by each suit.
Sevens so deplete the positive energies that they become
morally and physically weakened.

### Symbols associated with the number

✡ **Relation to the Suit:** Struggle upsetting the stability of the
   element

✡ **Sephira on the Tree of Life:** Netzach

# Eights ◯

### Keywords
SLOWING DOWN – PREPARATION FOR CHANGE –
WAIT – RE-EVALUATION – REVITALISATION

### Divinatory meaning
The energies are rebalanced and strengthened in the
eights as another energy brings them once again into
equilibrium. Eights represent a temporary success in one
area of the energies of each suit.

### Symbols associated with the number

✡ **Relation to the Suit:** Mastery and balance as represented
   by the element

✡ **Sephira on the Tree of Life:** Hod

# Nines

## Keywords
COMPREHENSION – CONSCIOUS – ACCEPTANCE –
UNDERSTANDING

## Divinatory meaning
Unlike the other odd numbers (apart from the ace), nines
remain in equilibrium. Indeed, nines become very stable,
representing a strong and stable force in the energies of
each suit.

## Symbols associated with the number

✡ **Relation to the Suit:** Fulfilment and completion of the
   element

✡ **Sephira on the Tree of Life:** Yesod

# Tens

## Keywords
TENSE – EXTREMES – ZENITH – NADIR –
COMPLETION

## Divinatory meaning
Tens are the peak of the energies embodied in each suit,
and represent completion. As with any absolute and
untempered force, tens create an imbalance in their
surroundings. Thus, ten is the only even number where
the energies are unstable. The excess in one energy leads
to a need to balance it with others, and indicates the
dissatisfaction inherent in any achievement.

## Symbols associated with the number

✡ **Relation to the Suit:** Completion of a cycle, preparing for a
   new cycle

✡ **Sephira on the Tree of Life:** Malkulth

# THE COURT CARDS

◆

## Girl

### Keywords
CURIOSITY – THE CHILD WITHIN – OPENNESS –
LIBERTY – FEARLESSNESS

### Divinatory meaning
The Girl represents the energy of each suit as expressed
through the curiosity of a child. The Girl needs to
understand and explore the world around her without
restrictions; she is full of carefree pleasure in the world
around her. The Girl represents being open, like a child,
to the fresh opportunities represented by the suit she is in.
All the images of the Boys and Girls on this deck of Tarot
cards are doubled. They represent the younger and less
stable energy they embody compared with the energy of
the Men and Women.

### Symbols associated with the card

✡ **World:** Assiah (The physical world and primal earth)

✡ **Element:** Earth

✡ **Energy:** Essence of the female spirit, energy as it is formed
on earth

✡ **Colour Scale:** Empress (black rayed with yellow)

✡ **Sephira on the Tree of Life:**
Malkulth, the crowned young
woman or virgin

# Boy

## Keywords
IMPULSE – DRIVING CHANGE – DESIRE –
CHANGEABILITY – STRUGGLE – CREATIVITY

## Divinatory meaning
The Boy represents the energy of each suit as expressed
through spiritual ideals. The Boy is dynamic and strong,
always rushing this way and that. However, unlike the
male energies found in the Man, the male energy of the
Boy is inexperienced and insecure. So the Boy blows and
buffets around like the wind on a stormy day; one
moment whirling around and creating eddies, the next
blowing so strongly that trees bend and crack, yet the
next moment hardly blowing at all, as if frightened by its
own power. Thus, the Boy represents energy acting upon
others in a dynamic, yet unstable, way.

## Symbols associated with the card

✿ **World:** Yetzirah (the formative world and primal air)

✿ **Element:** Air

✿ **Energy:** The essence of the male spirit

✿ **Colour Scale:** Emperor (rich salmon pink)

✿ **Sephira on the Tree of Life:**
Tipareth, the son, in the Messiah
centre, the place from where
mankind's spiritual ideals are created

# Woman

### Keywords
CREATIVITY – RESPONSIBILITY – CALMNESS –
DEEP UNDERSTANDING – CLARITY – HEALING

### Divinatory meaning
The Woman represents the energy of each suit as
expressed through creativity and emotional understanding, again tempered by responsibility and past
experience of deep love and sorrow. The energy of the
Woman is that of calm water; she is fluid, intuitive and
creative, seemingly still, but with strong currents running
underneath the surface.

### Symbols associated with the card

✡ **World:** Briah (the creative world and primal water)

✡ **Element:** Water

✡ **Energy:** Essence of the female spirit, which she turns into
the first form and which, although solid, still remains in
flux, like water

✡ **Colour Scale:** Queen (black)

✡ **Sephira on the Tree of Life:**
Binah, the Supernal Mother
and the receptacle of the
energy from Chokmah

# Man

## Keywords
RATIONAL – STABLE – STRONG – RESPONSIBLE –
DETERMINED – POWERFUL

## Divinatory meaning
The Man represents the energy of each suit as expressed
within the structures of success, power and social
responsibility. The energy of the Man is fiery, dynamic
and strong. Because of his age and experience, the Man's
energy is controlled and put to use in one direction. Thus,
he is rational, stable and pure.

## Symbols associated with the card

✡ **World**: Atziluth (pure spirit and primal fire)

✡ **Element:** Fire

✡ **Energy:** The essence of the male spirit

✡ **Colour Scale:** King (pure soft blue)

✡ **Sephira on the Tree of Life:**
   Chokmah, the Supernal Father
   and the original movement

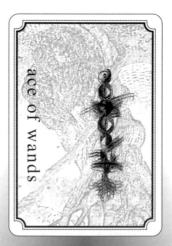

# THE MINOR ARCANA

◆

## Ace of Wands

### Keywords
DIVINE WILL – BREAKTHROUGH – CREATIVE POWER –
EXCEPTIONAL ENERGY – GOAL-ORIENTED –
TRANSFORMATION – PLEASURE AND STRUCTURE

### Divinatory meaning
Like a bolt out of the blue, you find yourself fired up to
take on new projects. New ideas enliven you. You
become inspired by life and new experiences. Optimism
drives you to new heights and saturates all areas of your
life.

### Advice
Draw another card from the deck to find out more about
what is inspiring you.

## Concept of the card

The Ace of Wands represents the manifestation of the will of the divine in
the individual. This dual image on the card is of the macro and microcosm.

The macro is what is visible, the Tree of Life. This tree grows and
blossoms, greening then wilting to the seasons of our planet. It provides a
marker in our environment, locating us in time and space.

Superimposed over the tree is a magical wand, a mixture between a
living tree with its roots spreading out beneath it, and a wand. Encircling
this wand is the double helix of DNA, the blueprint of life. This image
resembles the two snakes wound round the wand of Mercury, the
caduceus. This wand describes the micro, or what is invisible. It represents
the process of growth whereby the tree takes up and transforms the
energies locked in the soil into structure and life, and the energy of the sun
into colour and life. Many thousands of cells waltz through this wand in a
hidden dance, building and growing. The product of this dance, whose
rhythms are so microscopic we cannot see them with the human eye, is a
growth that is inexorable, but so slow that we are unable to see its end,
even in many human lifetimes.

# Two of Wands

## Keywords
ACHIEVEMENT – BALANCE – POWER – FOUNDATION –
ACTIVE CONTROL – FAITH IN THE FUTURE

## Divinatory meaning
You have built the foundations and your first plans have
been fulfilled. You are now in a position to take stock of
where you want to go in the future. You are restless and
looking for a change. Your energy is doubled, your
foundation is strong, and the ground is prepared for
future growth.

## Advice
Use your past experience to create your future.

# Concept of the card

This card represents symmetry in colour and form. The image has
been manipulated to balance dark and light, monochrome
representing the mental and colour representing the physical. The
inverted tree on the card forms a portal, a vessel for emotion. The
vines flow out and down from above, signifying the movement of
spirit.

## Symbols associated with the card

✡ **Esoteric Title:** Lord of Dominion

✡ **Astrology:** Mars in Aries

# Three of Wands

## Keywords
RECOGNITION – CLARIFY AREAS OF CONFLICT –
INNER VALUES – HONESTY – VIRTUE – WISDOM

## Divinatory meaning
You are in a well-established position and any attacks
from the outside are easily repelled. There is no need for
anxieties or worries. You now have the space to examine
your personal needs and to be honest about yourself, your
role in the world and how you deal with other people.
This is not the end-point in your career; you will soon
move onwards again, but with a new understanding of
your needs and motives and how best to achieve them.

## Advice
Occasionally check your perceptions of the world and
alter those which no longer fit.

# Concept of the card

The trunk of the tree on this card stands firm and strong. It is
well-established and its growth is mature. Now is the time to
examine the tree's interior, to check for minute weaknesses which
might prove to be a fatal flaw. The tree trunk and the image's
background have been sectioned and altered. All that you see is
contained within the original image, yet differences have
occurred. This is to illustrate how our perceptions of the world
around us are created internally and change frequently.

## Symbols associated with the card

✿ **Esoteric Title:** Lord of Established Strength

✿ **Astrology:** Sun in Aries

# Four of Wands

## Keywords
COMPLETION – HARMONY – HAVEN – ACCEPTANCE –
SPACE FROM WHICH TO MOVE FORWARD –
HARVEST-HOME – RESOLUTION

## Divinatory meaning
This card represents the idea of the harvest-home within the cyclic pattern of life. It indicates beginning, growth, harvest, celebration, rest and preparation. The harvest-home is the festival marking the close of harvest. It is a time of peace and celebration, when a community comes together to celebrate the harvest that has just been brought in.

When the Four of Wands appears in a reading, it could indicate a party being held to celebrate an important achievement in your life. You may be about to go on holiday or take time off from work and relax. It may simply mean that you are experiencing a harmonious and happy time at home. It can also mean moving into a new home.

## Advice
Remember that before you celebrate, you need to have completed any unfinished business.

# Concept of the card

The image of the tree on this card represents your mental and spiritual energies at the moment. Through the boughs of the tree a white light burns, presenting you with the gifts of clarity and vision and allowing you to see the external structure of your life clearly and objectively.

The cross is the balance in your life at the moment, and its four lines divide the image into four sections. These are the four elements or the four points of a compass, and they represent a completion.

The lines of the cross join together in the middle to create a single point. You are the centre of this cross and it represents the point from which you can move forwards.

## Symbols associated with the card

✿ **Esoteric Title:** Lord of Perfected Work

✿ **Astrology:** Venus in Aries

# Five of Wands

### Keywords
BURDEN – BLOCKED ENERGY – LOSS OF ENERGY –
RECOGNISE AND IMPLEMENT CHANGE – RELAX –
PROBLEMS – STRUGGLE – SLOW DOWN –
KEEP FOCUSED

### Divinatory meaning
This card indicates that you appear to be struggling with external forces, trying to prove yourself against what seems to be a greater force. The appearance of this card in a reading signifies that you are ready to tackle the situation. Many challenges appear in your life, but despite putting up an immense amount of effort, you may become weakened and anxious about failure.

### Advice
Look again at your situation and the problems you are fighting against: are they really that important? Indeed, are they real problems, or merely reflections of your own inner psyche? It is likely that if you relax a little and focus on solving problems one at a time, they will lose their power over you and you will overcome them. Draw another card from the deck to find a positive way through your problem or to discover what will happen when you tackle it. Let go, and let the force of nature flow through you.

## Concept of the card

The background of this card is solid, heavy grey. It represents the blockage caused by internal fears and depression magnifying external problems. The image of the tree is broken up and then divided into five sections which no longer connect with one another. This represents a weakening of force within you as a result of these blockages. But from the chasms between the wands comes a bright green light, the energy of new hope and new life.

### Symbols associated with the card

✿ **Esoteric Title:** Lord of Strife

✿ **Astrology:** Saturn in Leo

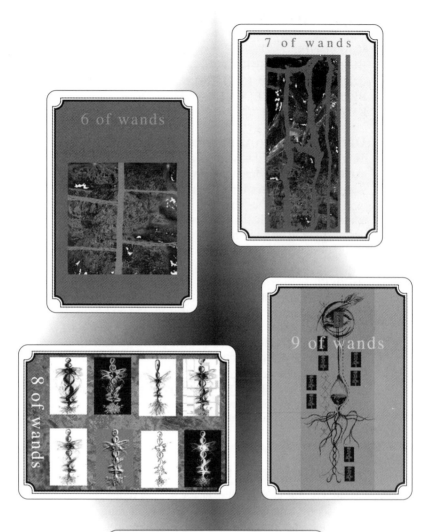

# Six of Wands

### Keywords
VICTORY – PROOF – SELF-CONFIDENCE – CLARITY –
STRENGTH – SUCCESS – LUCK – REVITALISATION

### Divinatory meaning
Self-confidence brings an awareness of the achievements
you have already made in your life. Indeed, you may have
just been rewarded in some way or have recently been
recognised for these achievements. This brings about an
optimistic frame of mind, which revitalises you and gives
you the clarity of thought to direct your energies into
finding solutions for other problems.

### Advice
Your optimism is catching and can be communicated to
others. If you share out your good fortune in this way
your happiness is bound to multiply.

## Concept of the card

In this card we are zooming in on the image of the tree at what
appears to be sub-atomic level, watching the sap rise. The
background of the card is a warm purple. High-energy orange
lines, representing self-confidence, seep through the solid
foundation created by the brick-like pattern of the wands.

### Symbols associated with the card

✡ **Esoteric Title:** Lord of Victory

✡ **Astrology:** Jupiter in Leo

# Seven of Wands

### Keywords
POWER – VALOUR – FAITH – WARRIOR – TRUTH –
RUSHING IN WHERE ANGELS FEAR TO TREAD –
HONEST AND OPEN CONFLICT

### Divinatory meaning
The Seven of Wands can mean standing up for what you
believe in, forcing revolutionary change in your
environment and maintaining your position against
opposition. When this card appears in a reading there is
likely to be conflict of some kind.

### Advice
Despite the odds appearing to be against you, you have
the strength to overcome your opponents, as long as you
are honest and unafraid.

# Concept of the card

Six wands criss-cross the rectangle of the tree in the centre of this
card, but one wand stands upright outside it. The rectangular box
becomes a single large wand opposing the much thinner one
beside it. Hence, this card represents having the courage to stand
up against overwhelming odds. The purple of the larger wand
opposes the brighter pink wand. This signifies authority opposing
valour and courage. In the end, the smaller wand transforms into
the larger wand, and becomes a warrior holding a spear.

### Symbols associated with the card

✡ **Esoteric Title:** Lord of Valour

✡ **Astrology:** Mars in Leo

# Eight of Wands

### Keywords
MOVEMENT – COMMUNICATION – HONESTY –
CLARIFICATION – DEFINE BOUNDARIES – PROGRESS

### Divinatory meaning
Restlessness and movement of thought start discussions
and ideas flowing. New honesty and openness in
communication will free up old problems and allow you
to move on. This card also indicates the passage of time
moving swiftly on to the next phase. Therefore, when the
card comes between two separate incidents it shows
that the transformation from one situation to the other
comes quickly.

### Advice
Be aware that this card often indicates speedy change
from one event to another. It does not necessarily
describe a situation itself.

## Concept of the card
The illustration on this card depicts eight rectangles of
monochrome colour, each representing old blockages. The image
of the ace, however, is spinning within each rectangle. The ace's
movement breaks up the old misunderstandings and problems
which have stood in your way and reveals the rainbow clarity
behind them.

### Symbols associated with the card

✡ **Esoteric Title:** Lord of Swiftness

✡ **Astrology:** Mercury in Sagittarius

# Nine of Wands

### Keywords
PROTECTIVE INNER STRENGTH – POWER –
HEALTHY IMMUNE SYSTEM – FULL CONSCIOUSNESS –
EXPAND YOUR BOUNDARIES WITHOUT FEAR –
GROWTH

### Divinatory meaning
Your understanding of a situation and your instinctual
reactions to it are one and the same. This gives you the
strength of belief to tackle problems in the correct way.
Your conscious mind is given the chance to see what is in
the subconscious mind. Old fears and paranoias appear,
but at this time you can easily overcome them. You find
the strength within yourself to grow beyond old
boundaries.

### Advice
You have the inner strength to break through old personal
boundaries. Do not try to retreat back into them just
because they are familiar and safe. If you do, you may be
missing a great opportunity to experience more of life.

## Concept of the card

The background on this card is derived from a mix of deep pink
and white and refers to womb and sperm, feminine and
masculine. The roots of the subconscious self spread out from the
bulb, or seed, at the centre. The bulb or seed is also like an
alchemical retort, the glass container containing the fluid seed,
the aqua vitae. This water of life grows upwards to feed the plant,
whose flower is the all-seeing eye or conscious self.

The nine wands are divided into four groups of two, each
representing a different stage of the mechanical process of
growth. The last wand covers the flower of this process: an
understanding of oneself, or the power gained when both the
conscious and subconscious self are working together.

### Symbols associated with the card

✡ **Esoteric Title:** Lord of Great Strength

✡ **Astrology:** Sun in Sagittarius

# Ten of Wands

### Keywords
DO NOT ALLOW RESTRICTION – SELF-REPRESSION –
SEPARATION – LOSS OF COMMUNICATION –
FEAR OF REJECTION, PUNISHMENT OR SHAME –
ENJOY – FREE YOURSELF

### Divinatory meaning
You feel bound and tied down by heavy burdens. These
burdens repress you and separate you from your free and
happy self inside. You feel unable to communicate your
desire to be free, because you are afraid that you will be
letting others down or that you will be punished for not
being able to carry on.

### Advice
Do not be afraid to express yourself. Dare to break out
and voice your fears and hopes to others; you will find
that they will respect you, understand you and help to
ease your burdens. Draw another card from the deck to
find a positive way through your problem or an indication
of what will happen when you tackle it.

## Concept of the card

The black background of this card symbolises the darkness of
oppression, the oblivion we fear and the despair we feel. The tree
on this card is broken up; its powers are flowing disjointedly and
the wrong way. The wands crossing the tree are blue, indicating
that the blockage comes from the intellect.

### Symbols associated with the card

✡ **Esoteric Title:** Lord of Oppression

✡ **Astrology:** Saturn in Sagittarius

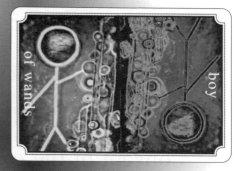

# Girl of Wands

### Keywords
TRANSLATION OF FEAR INTO LOVE –
DEATH OF FEAR – NEWNESS – STRENGTH

### Divinatory meaning
This card heralds the overcoming of old fears with a new vision of life, regaining childish innocence and openness. It often indicates being told of new and exciting projects. If the card refers to a person, it represents someone in touch with the child within. They are willing to try anything new and enjoy being busy. They are straight-forward and uncomplicated like a child, although they are often unable to stay still for long. They chop and change as new ideas pass through their mind.

### Advice
This card traditionally represents a message. Whatever the actual message is, it is in fact a gift. An initiate is often told a secret word or given a new understanding of the word; in the same way this card represents the gift of a key to a new life. This gift will help you to transform darkness into light, and fear into love.

## Concept of the card

The Girl on this card looks you in the face, partially clad and holding a wand. She is heavily pregnant, and about to become a mother; she is about to experience an initiation. Within her belly she holds a universe of stars. The background of the card is divided into black and white parts. This represents the Girl's hopes and fears about the future, both spiritually and physically. The initiation and birth will bring her face to face with her fears and it will help her overcome these fears.

### Symbols associated with the card

✪ **Esoteric Titles:** Princess of the Shining Flame – Rose of the Palace of Fire

✪ **Elements:** Earthy aspect of fire

# Boy of Wands

## Keywords
DRIVING CHANGE – FREEDOM – CREATIVITY –
LIGHT AND LOVE WITHOUT LIMIT –
LOVE OF LIFE

## Divinatory meaning
This card represents a sudden impulsive desire to do
something, to break out of a stagnant situation. With it
come excitement and passion for an idea. People
represented by the Boy of Wands are passionate and
impatient, with a tendency to act first and think later.
They want to be on the move all the time. At their worst,
they can be aggressive and blind to criticism or other
people's wishes; at their best, they invigorate those
around them and can achieve much.

## Advice
Don't let yourself be contained, for life is prepared to
receive you.

# Concept of the card

The Boy on this card is a pioneer. He holds a magical staff, the
staff of life, clustered around which are sperm. These sperm are
glowing with myriad colours of magical energy, the drive to
create life. The Boy blazes with an energy that is radioactive; it
melts and blisters, but does not hurt.

## Symbols associated with the card

✿ **Esoteric Title:** Prince of the Chariot of Fire

✿ **Elements:** Airy aspect of fire

# Woman of Wands

## Keywords
COMPASSION – SELF-COMPREHENSION –
RECOGNITION OF EMOTIONS – TEACHER –
HEALER – COMMUNICATION – MEMORIES

## Divinatory meaning
This card indicates success in situations requiring emotional strength, drive and creativity. Your self-belief and experience will carry out your visions. People represented by the Woman of Wands are sincere, warm and strong. They have a calm, reassuring presence and are full of creative ideas. They are able to intuit other people's desires and visions, and they have the experience to know how to fulfil these visions. They will fight hard when obstructed.

## Advice
You are right to fight hard to help others, because you know intimately the pain and loss life can bring. The gift of creativity and understanding this card represents is not just given to you to make you feel good, you should also use it to help others.

# Concept of the card

A Woman squats low in the illustration on this card, her pregnant belly pressing her down. Her arms are folded behind her. The warm nut-red of her body stands out against the watery background. She is the feeling of heat and wetness; her moist belly is the fiery crucible of creativity from which her spirit radiates.

In front of the Woman is an image of herself, small and crystal clear, representing understanding and compassion for others through experience and memory. Her eyes are closed as she concentrates on the feelings burning inside. She is intuition and understanding of the creation; she knows that she and the child in her belly are one. She radiates her powerful calm over others, transforming people emotionally.

## Symbols associated with the card

✤ **Esoteric Title:** Queen of the Throne of Flames

✤ **Elements:** Watery aspect of fire

# Man of Wands

## Keywords
DYNAMISM – PERCEPTION – BURNING ENERGY –
DECISION-MAKING IN THE PHYSICAL WORLD –
OPTIMISM – VISION

## Divinatory meaning
This card expresses a deliberate action, positive and
forceful, behind which is a vision of the goal to be
gained. It signifies the burning away of negativity and
ambitions. People represented by the Man of Wands are
enthusiastic, calm, organised, honest and strong. When
they want something done, they can also be stubborn,
interfering and bullying, without realising the effect they
have on others.

## Advice
You are like a new-born child who knows what you want
and how to get it. Like the newborn, you already have all
you need. Do not constrict yourself or worry about where
you are going. Your vision is true; all you have to do is
grow into it.

# Concept of the card

The Man on this card is seated, half on land and half on water;
behind him is a fleshy, pearly spiral. He raises his right hand to
use his wand; his thoughts are strongly directed, flowing through
his body to be enacted on the physical. His eyes are closed,
emphasising the strength and power of the inner will. He is the
leader; he has the experience to know that he is right. The energy
the Man of Wands controls is positive and fiery, burning away all
obstructions in his path.

## Symbols associated with the card

✡ **Esoteric Titles:** Lord of the Flame and of Lightning –
King of the Spirits of Fire

✡ **Elements:** Fiery aspect of fire

ace of cups

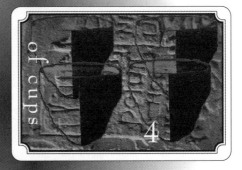

3 of cups

# Ace of Cups

### Keywords
ALL-ENCOMPASSING LOVE – OVERFLOWING LOVE –
THE BALANCE OF EMOTIONS – SELF-ACCEPTANCE –
GENEROSITY OF SPIRIT

### Divinatory meaning
When the Ace of Cups is dealt you are experiencing the
joy and happiness of all-encompassing, overflowing and
unconditional love. Aleister Crowley calls this card 'the
universal orgasm'. It indicates internal joy and love –
whether it be love of the physical world around you, the
joy of a job well done, a new friendship or lover, the birth
of a child, or the love of your own parents. This love
brings about a new atmosphere in your life. As well as
receiving love, you distribute love at this time; love
affects everything you do.

### Advice
Let the joy of your love flow into every part of your life
to illuminate the world around you.

## Concept of the card
The cup on this card represents the fluid side of ourselves, a side
which cannot be analysed or pinned down, but which is liquid and
ever-changing, it represents our emotions. The Ace of Cups holds
our dreams and embodies our core emotions. These seep into all
parts of our lives; they are hidden, yet supporting; they nourish us
and cleanse us like blood.

The image depicted on the card is a snapshot into the multi-
faceted, but always connected, global network of relationships.
We all come from one pot, one grail, one womb. Two runic
magpies fly through the wisps of mist and rays of light. Seeds turn
into leaves and are carried off by the wind. In the centre of the
image is one big, swirling, organic cauldron. Its physical form is
very like a hair follicle or a sweat gland. It represents the unseen
seepages and connections which physically link us all. Telepathy,
like falling in love, should be as easy as catching the common
cold.

# Two of Cups

## Keywords
PARTNERSHIP – CO-OPERATION – LOVING UNION –
DEEPLY DEVELOPING RELATIONSHIPS – JOY – BLISS

## Divinatory meaning
This card describes the experience of a partnership
between two people – whether it be a love affair,
friendship or working as a team. You and another are able
to give and receive good things and to share your
experience of the world on a deep emotional level.

## Advice
The Two of Cups has a similar meaning to the Lovers
card of the Major Arcana. However, it is the beginning of
love, rather than the mature and full expression of love
represented by the Lovers. The Two of Cups is an internal
balancing, or mixing, of the male and female energies
inside oneself. In other words, it is about learning to love
yourself. After reaching the stage of loving oneself, an
external partnership often quickly follows.

# Concept of the card

The two white tea cups illustrated on the card remind us of the
cosiness and happiness of sharing a cup of tea with someone. The
cups sit, handles together, as if they are holding hands. They are
empty, ready to be filled.

Underneath the cups is a yellow and green mandala based on
the Rosy Cross, the emblem of the Rosicrucians, and a star to
signify recognition and comprehension. Experiencing love is
another way to feel the joy of universal consciousness. The
colours green and yellow predominate in this card, reminding us
of the colours of the daffodil and the vibrant energy and newness
of spring. Green is also sacred to Venus, the goddess of love. On
the outside of each cup is a pair of people, both exhibiting and
sharing the joy and happiness of love.

## Symbols associated with the card

✿ **Esoteric Title:** Lord of Love

✿ **Astrology:** Venus in Cancer

# Three of Cups

### Keywords
CELEBRATION – EXCEPTIONAL LOVE – HONOUR –
VERY SPECIAL PEOPLE IN YOUR LIFE – INTIMACY –
FRIENDSHIP – LOYALTY

### Divinatory meaning
The Three of Cups heralds a time of celebration and joy.
It may mean a reunion with friends or family. It is the
sense of abundance and well-being that relationships
with family and friends can bring.

### Advice
Share your love freely with a small group of intimate
friends.

## Concept of the card

On this card the energy between the three cups is so strong that
they have started to melt together, their contents mixing up,
pouring out and forming a blue spiritual light. This card
represents very personal and intimate unions; it represents
melding, supporting and strengthening relationships. The Three
of Cups is the card of friendships, celebrations and parties.

### Symbols associated with the card

✡ **Esoteric Title:** Lord of Abundance

✡ **Astrology:** Mercury in Cancer

# Four of Cups

## Keywords
EMOTIONAL BLOCKAGE AND CONFUSION –
DISCONTENT WITH THOSE YOU LOVE –
DO NOT ALLOW RESTRICTIONS TO BE IMPOSED –
DO NOT BECOME DEPENDENT OR SUFFOCATING –
EMOTIONAL SECURITY – DO NOT LOSE YOUR SENSITIVITY

## Divinatory meaning
You are lucky enough to be well-loved and cared for, and you have an abundance of emotional security. However, there is a sense of dissatisfaction with a relationship: you have perhaps become too dependent on it, and it has lost its magic. Your reaction to this is to try to stop the love (which seems suffocating) from flowing in your direction. You do this by cutting yourself off from its source. Arguments become your main form of communication, and you start dreaming of escape.

## Advice
When you recognise that your dreams of escape come from a blockage on your part, you can learn to re-create these dreams in the reality of your relationship. Draw another card from the deck to find a positive way through your problem or to find what will happen when you tackle it.

# Concept of the card
The natural state of emotion is fluid; it should flow back and forth between people. If you hold on to any emotion too tightly it begins to solidify and take on the qualities of stone. It will become outwardly secure and strong, yet internally it will become heavy and rough. Relationships will seem inflexible, and life will become grey and colourless. When you cut yourself off from those you love, communication becomes as difficult as reading the undeciphered inscription on this stone from an eleventh-century Welsh building. Thus, the only emotion you can express is as angry as the red liquid the cups contain. The partial coloration and semi-opacity of the cups on this card relates to the choices you have to make. You may choose to make these cups either completely solid or completely transparent.

## Symbols associated with the card

✿ **Esoteric Title:** Lord of Blended Pleasure

✿ **Astrology:** Moon in Cancer

# Five of Cups

## Keywords
REGRET – PESSIMISM – FEAR OF DISAPPOINTMENT –
HOPES AND EXPECTATIONS DEFLATED –
LEARN FROM YOUR DISAPPOINTMENTS AND DO
NOT REPEAT THEM

## Divinatory meaning
Your expectations of someone or something have been
proved to be wrong, or you are afraid that they will be
proved so. This card represents a process of grieving over
a future you feel is lost. It can also represent a separation
from someone you love, or a loss of trust in a
relationship. As a result you have become pessimistic and
have stopped believing that life can bring you good
things. Once the grieving process is over, your spirits will
rise up again.

## Advice
Draw another card from the deck to find a positive way
through your problem or to discover what will happen
when you tackle it.

# Concept of the card

There are five cups in this card's illustration, but only one catches
your eye. It is the fragile and empty glass cup that is turned over.
It can no longer hold your hopes and expectations of love and
happiness. The black words on its surface no longer tell you of the
joys of life, but distort and block out the wealth of love held in the
cups beneath. Look, however, through this cup's transparent
surface to the cups below. Not all is lost; they have caught most
of the liquid flowing from the empty cup above.

The left-hand cornerstone of this precarious arrangement
of crockery is inscribed with stanza five from Lord Byron's
*Don Juan*:

> Marriage from love, like vinegar from wine
> A sad, sour sober beverage – by time

## Symbols associated with the card

✡ **Esoteric Title:** Lord of Loss in Pleasure

✡ **Astrology:** Mars in Scorpio

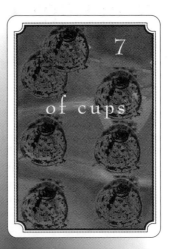

# Six of Cups

## Keywords
PLEASURE – PAST PAINS ARE FORGOTTEN –
SEXUALITY – READINESS TO MEET A PARTNER –
SENSUALITY

## Divinatory meaning
This card represents a time of open and giving love,
which you experience as if for the first time. Indeed, it
sometimes means that an old lover has re-entered the
scene. Whoever you are attracted to, you are open and
receptive to sharing your happiness with others again.
The enticing sensations of lust, love and passion rise to
the surface.

## Advice
This card often represents what at first may seem to be
taking an emotional risk. In reality, the relationship will
be one in which trust and unconditional giving will be as
natural as breathing.

# Concept of the card

The feather of a peacock, the bird of luxury and pleasure is the
background to this illustration of the Six of Cups. The feather is
like a warm sun, radiating restorative energies into your mind,
body and soul. It is as if you have been outside on a cold day and
come in to a warm fire. It is only as the heat of the fire enters your
body and you slowly warm up that you realise how little you have
been able to feel. Sensation comes flooding back, first into your
fingers and then your hands, and you start being able to move
again.

## Symbols associated with the card

✡ **Esoteric Title:** Lord of Pleasure

✡ **Astrology:** Sun in Scorpio

# Seven of Cups

## Keywords
OVER-INDULGENCE – DEBAUCHERY – MISUSE OF
PLEASURE, EMOTION OR CREATIVITY –
DISORGANISATION – LACK OF FOCUS –
USUAL PLEASURES SEEM TIRED AND SORDID

## Divinatory meaning
On a basic level you appear to have an exciting and
fulfilling life, but there is an over-abundance preventing
you from focusing on and enjoying life's pleasures.
Everything seems too much; and things which you would
have grasped at with both hands and enjoyed to the full,
now seem empty and stale. This is because you are trying
to do too much.

## Advice
Be honest with yourself. Slow down and cut back what
you are doing to the things that are really important to
you. Draw another card from the deck to find a positive
way through your particular problem or to find what will
happen when you tackle it.

# Concept of the card

The background of the cups on this card is foggy brown and
green. It symbolises being lost in the fog of emotions, unable to
see what you want to do or a way out. All the cups are upside
down and empty, a denial of their basic function. Moreover, they
are made of fragile glass. This represents having too much to do,
too many dreams, too many emotions. It signifies that everything
you do seems to be shallow and unfulfilling.

## Symbols associated with the card

✡ **Esoteric Title:** Lord of Illusory Success

✡ **Astrology:** Venus in Scorpio

# Eight of Cups

## Keywords
EXHAUSTION – WASTED EMOTIONAL ENERGY –
FOCUSING EMOTIONS OUTSIDE YOURSELF –
BOREDOM – STAGNATION – FOCUSING EMOTIONS
TOWARDS PEOPLE WHO ARE UNABLE TO GIVE LOVE
IN RETURN

## Divinatory meaning
You have been expending a lot of time and emotion on a
situation that is no longer fulfilling. It has been like
trying to fill a bottomless well: the more you put in, the
less it gives. So now you are walking away. The balance
of the scales has finally tipped. You are free to turn your
back and leave, knowing that you do not owe anyone
anything.

## Advice
You did your best; it is now time to move on. Draw
another card from the deck to find a positive way through
your problem or to discover what will happen when you
tackle it.

# Concept of the card

The illustration on this card depicts a barren landscape. It
signifies that you have a choice. You can walk to the chair and sit
down, becoming part of the landscape, drained of life, isolated
and numb. Or you can take the horse and ride out of this desert.

## Symbols associated with the card

✧ **Esoteric Title:** Lord of Abandoned Success

✧ **Astrology:** Saturn in Pisces

# Nine of Cups

## Keywords
JOY – STRENGTH – ECSTASY – BALANCE –
TRUE HAPPINESS

## Divinatory meaning
The Nine of Cups brings with it a great sense of joy and
happiness, from both material and emotional well-being.
Life is good and love is strong. You have what you need
to be happy and you feel rooted and secure in your
environment.

## Advice
The cup of love is full and overflowing; do not let natural
pessimism turn it over. Take this time to enjoy yourself –
you deserve it.

# Concept of the card
The cups illustrated on this card are in the shape of a sunflower:
eight of the cups form the stalk and leaves, and the ninth cup (on
which is written the poem from the Universe) is the flower itself.
The ninth cup is centred on the mandala, which radiates, like a
sun, communicating the sense of emotional happiness and well-
being this card represents. This card reveals one of the clues to
how to be happy. Because the cup is made of glass, it can either
look as if it is facing up and holding in love, or facing down and
empty. Therefore, whether you think the cup is half-full or half-
empty is a matter of perception.

## Symbols associated with the card

✡ **Esoteric Title:** Lord of Material Happiness

✡ **Astrology:** Jupiter in Pisces

# Ten of Cups

## Keywords
SATISFACTION – COMPLETE EXPRESSION –
PERFECT, ILLUMINATING AND SELF-SUFFICIENT LOVE –
AWARENESS OF LOVE

## Divinatory meaning
With the Ten of Cups you have found your emotional
Eden. It represents having a good relationship with
everyone around you. Even old enemies smile at you and
become happy in your presence. You become aware of the
love surrounding you every day. Sometimes when this
card appears it means being in a lasting, happy
relationship; it can even represent marriage. But
regardless of whether the love comes from a partner or
family and friends, it is a time of being deeply in touch
with your emotions and being blessed by the knowledge
of just how much love you have around you.

## Advice
You have all you need to be happy. Enjoy.

# Concept of the card

This illustration reminds us that we have cups of every kind in our
life. They spiral upwards on the card, towards the centrally placed
inscribed cup. Spillages do not matter – there is more than enough
love to share out. The affirmation of the Nine of Cups that 'you
have everything you need to be happy', is handwritten across the
card. The white, pink and yellow colours combine to create a rosy
glow. The inscribed cup is placed centrally on the mandala, but
rests above the still water of emotions. The sunflower cups are a
direct reference to the sun and represent heat, heart and energy.

## Symbols associated with the card

✡ **Esoteric Title:** Lord of Perfected Success

✡ **Astrology:** Mars in Pisces

# Girl of Cups

## Keywords
DEATH OF JEALOUSY – EMOTIONAL LIBERTY –
SELF-WORTH – HUMOUR – GENTLENESS –
TENDERNESS – FREEDOM – SELF-LOVE

## Divinatory meaning
The Girl of Cups heralds a time when you have access,
through meditation and imagination, to your dreams and
desires. If you have psychic ability, it rises to the surface
and allows you to explore freely the astral levels for
creative, artistic and self-contemplative ends. This is also
a time when you are emotionally open to the possibility
of love. Indeed, it is often a time when you receive a
message from, or meet, a new lover.

People represented by the Girl of Cups are dreamers,
able to live in the worlds of imagination and reality at one
and the same time. They are child-like in love, open
emotionally to others and able to give and receive love
freely. However, they are not yet ready to settle down and
accept commitment or responsibility; to them, love is still
a romantic comedy.

## Advice
Listen to your heart and be ready to see everyone in a
new light.

# Concept of the card

In the illustration on this card a Girl holds up the cup of emotion,
offering it freely as she looks to the stars. She has conquered her
lower self, she has won over jealousy and possessiveness, and
now gives her love openly. Her lower self, although still animal,
has been transformed into a swift horse, giving her freedom to
travel wherever she wants.

## Symbols associated with the card

✿ **Esoteric Title:** Princess of Water and the Lotus

✿ **Elements:** Earthy aspect of water

# Boy of Cups

### Keywords
DESIRES – ILLUSIONS – CHANGE – POTENTIAL –
HARNESSING OF SEXUALITY AND PASSION –
FREEDOM – FULFILMENT

### Divinatory meaning
This card signifies feeling trapped, with the need to break
free from responsibility to others, and to change the
situation around you. You may be experiencing strong
sexual fantasies at this time, or you are being driven by
your need to feel that you are in command of your
emotions. You think that you are in control; but it is your
suppressed emotions that are controlling you.

People represented by the Boy of Cups can be gentle,
sensitive and idealistic – but afraid of their own
vulnerability in love. This means that on the surface they
have a tendency to repress their emotions. When such a
person is particularly stressed, they may express love as
overwhelming sexual desire. If these people are stressed,
they may approach all aspects of life as a power struggle
in which they use deception against themselves and
others.

### Advice
If you break out and contact your innermost fears and
emotions, you will transform your life. You will thus gain
emotional fulfilment and an understanding of yourself
and others.

## Concept of the card
On this card a boy stands in front of the blue and green squares of
the material world, the figures hidden in the squares representing
action and work. He looks both left and right, but his vision is not
focused directly ahead. Above him are his dreams, vivid, pulsing
and racing in his veins, they are saturated pink with desires and
cravings. He harnesses these emotions to drive him on in his quest
for perceived power in the rational and material world.

### Symbols associated with the card

✡ **Esoteric Title:** Prince of the Chariot of Water

✡ **Elements:** Airy aspect of water

# Woman of Cups

## Keywords
BALANCE – REFLECTION – INTUITIVE EMPATHY –
EMOTIONAL UNDERSTANDING – MOTHER –
GENEROSITY – BIRTH AND REBIRTH

## Divinatory meaning
This card represents being in touch with your emotions in
a profound way. You are able to recognise the way love
touches and moulds all areas of your life and are able to
examine situations in relation to your emotional
motivations. It can be a time when you fall deeply in love
with someone. You may recognise your love for your
mother or experience the birth of a child.

People represented by the Woman of Cups have a
deep and mature link with their emotions and intuitive
sides. They react calmly and lovingly in all situations
because they understand their own and other people's
emotional sensitivities. They have the strength to care for
others, and to be a unifying force where there is discord,
because they do so without losing sight of their own
needs and desires. This is the experience of unconditional
love, as opposed to self-sacrifice.

## Advice
Do not be afraid to show your inner emotions openly.
Although some people may not understand you, there are
those who will benefit greatly from your compassion and
understanding.

# Concept of the card

In the illustration the Woman of Cups sits with that which is most
precious to her – her child – balanced, but unheld, on her lap. It is
her child who has crowned her, and her child who has given her
access to the deep well of her own emotions, which she now
offers to us in the golden chalice. She is bathed in a shimmering
golden light, reflected off the surface of the water held in the
chalice. She smiles internally and externally, aware of her
responsibilities.

## Symbols associated with the card

✡ **Esoteric Title:** Queen of the Thrones of Water

✡ **Elements:** Watery aspect of water

# Man of Cups

### Keywords
RESPONSIBILITY OF LOVE – FAMILY – SURRENDER –
EMOTIONAL ELEVATION – HUMILITY – FATHER –
HOPE OF PERFECTION

### Divinatory meaning
The Man of Cups represents relationships with a close
spiritual connection, such as within a family. It is about
fulfilling your emotional commitments and recognising
your love for your father. When the card appears in a
reading, you are likely to experience the ebb and flow of
emotion that creates mutual understanding.

If this card refers to a person, it represents someone
who is mature and wise, though perhaps not self-
obsessed or driven enough to make a good leader.
However, such people will wish to support and create a
happy atmosphere for those they love. Most importantly,
where necessary, they will sacrifice their own dreams and
desires because of this responsibility and love they feel
for others.

### Advice
To give love is to receive love; and to protect love is to be
protected by love.

# Concept of the card

On this card, a man, a father, sits in his home and firmly holds his
son in his arms. He knows the joy and warmth of all-
encompassing and protective love. The love he felt for his own
father as a child is the same love he feels now for his own son.

### Symbols associated with the card

✡ **Esoteric Titles:** Lord of the Waves and Waters – King of
the Hosts of the Sea

✡ **Elements:** Fiery aspect of water

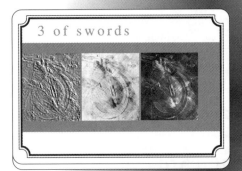

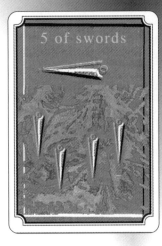

# Ace of Swords

### Keywords
PHENOMENAL CLARITY – BRILLIANT THINKING –
RECOGNITION – ABSOLUTE DECISIONS –
PERCEPTION – LIVING IN THE MOMENT – REALITY

## Divinatory meaning
When the Ace of Swords appears in a reading new ideas
and thoughts form. You are able to take on and solve
difficult problems with clarity and great rationality. You
can pierce through the misty fogs of emotion and push
aside apparently immovable obstacles to reach the truth
of a situation, the finding of which is almost like a
spiritual revelation. This card sometimes indicates an
internal physical illness requiring an operation.

## Advice
The sword will bring great clarity of thought into your
life; however, you should use your heart and compassion
to temper its blade. If you try to communicate all that you
now see so clearly, you may cut others deeply.

# Concept of the card

The energy of the sword comes from the intellect; it pierces, cuts
through and transforms. The image on this card is a composite,
representing objects which hold the same energy. A sword over
time may be a pen, a gun, a sickle or a hypodermic needle – all
these symbolise the way that thought can cut down and destroy
old structures and ideas to bring through the new.

# Two of Swords

## Keywords
TRANQUIL RELATIONSHIPS – PEACE – SERENITY –
SURRENDER – INNER FOCUS – CALM DECISIONS

## Divinatory meaning
You have been pushed and pulled around by problems,
and the amount of work you have had recently has not
allowed you to find time to think. Suddenly there is an
oasis of calm around you, and the issues you need to
tackle stand out clearly in front of you.

## Advice
If you make decisions about your life now, you will be
able to do so with an attitude of calm, and dispassionate
reason. It is always easier to see the solutions to other
people's problems, but at this moment in your life you are
lucky enough to be able to make choices about your own
life as if it were someone else's.

# Concept of the card

Two identical scenes confront us on this card, depicted in
complementary colours with equal tonal values. In each, a man
stands, arms folded, poised in front of what looks like a cannon
with smoke filling the air above. It is like a war scene. The shape
of the cannon shifts and changes the more you look at it; hidden
within is a gun, or even a tiger. The man stands beneath the
clouds, but above the moon, and stares through a telescope or
gunsight. There is no battle, and neither of the guns are facing one
another. It is a truce. The red blood spilt by the battle has mixed
with the green leaves of new hope, a new life. It signifies peace
from battle, the calm after the storm.

## Symbols associated with the card

✡ **Esoteric Title:** Lord of Peace Restored

✡ **Astrology:** Moon in Libra

# Three of Swords

### Keywords
NEGATIVE THINKING WORSENING THE SITUATION –
COMPLICATED RELATIONSHIPS – SORROW –
CONFUSION – THE NEED TO MAKE CLEAR CHOICES –
DECISIONS REGARDING RELATIONSHIPS – DOUBT –
MISFORTUNE OF OTHERS AFFECTING YOU
EMOTIONALLY

### Divinatory meaning
This card often indicates trouble in three-sided relationships. Something happens to you or to someone close to you, which creates an atmosphere of sorrow, grief and pain. Relationships become stressful, and painful decisions have to be made.

### Advice
It is important not only to see the dark side of the situation. Recognise and either accept or control negative thoughts. If you feel too weak to fight your grief, find a friend who can help you to your feet and enable you to see the sunny side of life again. Draw another card from the deck to find a positive way through your problem or to see what will happen when you tackle it.

# Concept of the card

The three sword symbols on this card each represent a different form of emotional disintegration. The black sword represents guilty sorrow. It is when you feel hollow, empty and black inside. You hate yourself and feel anger and guilt towards those you love. The white sword represents pallid grief. It is when you feel numb, both emotionally and physically. You feel insubstantial, as if you are fading away, and are light, like a feather. At this time you are not in control. The grey sword represents heavy pain. It is when you have been so hurt emotionally by others that it is as if you have been cut and scratched deep to your core. You feel so drained by your sadness that your emotions become heavy and slow and you cannot escape your pain.

### Symbols associated with the card

✡ **Esoteric Title:** Lord of Sorrow

✡ **Astrology:** Saturn in Libra

# Four of Swords

## Keywords
TRUCE – PROBLEMS NOT YET FULLY RESOLVED –
COMPROMISE – RECOVERY FROM ILLNESS –
REST – SURFACE CALM

## Divinatory meaning
This card represents a truce, rather than a battle won or a
problem solved. You are given a period of rest and
relaxation before the problems and tensions of your
recent past reappear again. Sometimes it indicates a
minor illness, like a cold or flu, which forces you to take
a break from your work and problems while your body
regains the strength to deal with them again.

## Advice
This period of rest will give you the chance to get matters
into perspective, so that you are less emotionally attached
to a particular outcome.

# Concept of the card

The four symbols of the sword on this card are in balance, with
the two vibrant swords and two dull swords facing their opposites
and balancing their pair in the corners. It represents stalemate or
a rest from the battle. However, once one side regains the upper
hand, they will regroup and the battle will recommence.

## Symbols associated with the card

✡ **Esoteric Title:** Lord of Rest from Strife

✡ **Astrology:** Jupiter in Libra

# Five of Swords

### Keywords
FEAR OF HELPLESSNESS – LOSS – DEFEAT –
NEGATIVE FEELINGS CREATED BY IRRATIONAL FEAR –
CLARIFY WHAT YOU ARE AFRAID OF – IMBALANCE –
FEAR IS ILLUSORY – RELAX

### Divinatory meaning
Someone or something has opened up old fears, and now
you see life as a battle or fight. You become afraid of
losing or becoming weakened, the effect of which is
paralysing.

### Advice
Remember that these fears come from within and are
related to past experiences and internal hopes and fears.
Loss or defeat is an attitude of mind experienced only by
you, and does not exist in reality. Draw another card from
the deck to find a positive way through your problem or
to discover what will happen when you tackle it.

## Concept of the card

On this card the sword of the self floats above four smaller
swords, which are being tossed about by a violent sea. The self is
isolated, unable to help or be helped. In fact it is safe, out of reach
of the waves, whilst the other swords, although battered, remain
upright and strong. Life is so dominated by fear that you become
embedded and fossilised in the moment. Change and fear become
so entangled in your mind you forget that without pain there is no
life. The yellow of the letters on this card is a reference to the light
and strong positive energy, which is always available if we need
or want it.

### Symbols associated with the card

✡ **Esoteric Title:** Lord of Defeat

✡ **Astrology:** Venus in Aquarius

6 of swords

7 of swords

8 of swords

9 of swords

10 of swords

# Six of Swords

### Keywords
ANALYTICAL – SUPER-CRITICAL – SUPER-LOGICAL –
VISIONARY – REVITALISATION – REVELATION –
DISCUSSION – COMMUNICATION

### Divinatory meaning
You have been working hard, building up skills and an
understanding of life, when suddenly you leap an
evolutionary stage or two, and your old ideas and beliefs
are blown apart by this new vision. This intellectual
transformation can affect the way you see yourself on a
professional, intellectual or emotional basis. It is
important that you communicate to others your ideas, and
the fact that you see the world differently, so that they too
can adjust to this change and help you bring your ideas to
fruition.

### Advice
You are tapping into ideas from the edge of
understanding. It is important that you communicate
these ideas to others, so that the momentum of change
and transformation is shared.

## Concept of the card

This card illustrates a bright, vibrant, new understanding or
realisation exploding in your mind and burning away the old
mental structures you have built up around you. This gives you a
new vision of life.

### Symbols associated with the card

✡ **Esoteric Title:** Lord of Earned Success

✡ **Astrology:** Mercury in Aquarius

# Seven of Swords

## Keywords
DESPAIR – CONFUSION – EXHAUSTION –
INCONSTANCY – NEGATIVITY – PRESSURE –
TONGUE-TIED – FUTILITY –
DO NOT TRAP YOURSELF

## Divinatory meaning
You are mentally exhausted at the moment. Too many
things are happening and you can no longer hold them all
in your mind; it becomes impossible to see where you are
going. This causes a feeling of powerlessness and lack of
control, which in turn leads you to redouble your efforts
in order to try to remain in control. In reality you are fine.

## Advice
Recognise the real cause of your confusion and lack of
control. Give yourself a break. Do not become trapped by
too many unrealistic expectations of yourself. Draw another
card from the deck to find a positive way through your
problem or to see what will happen when you tackle it.

# Concept of the card

The background of this card is a radioactive, fluorescent swirl of
disparate colours, on which the white text is fighting to be seen.
This represents a lack of mental clarity. Opportunities and
possibilities appear and disappear out of the mist of indecision
and confusion you feel. The seven swords are represented by
seven hollow tweezer-like implements, representing the anxiety
and paranoia you feel. Success seems to keep slipping out of your
grasp; it is as if you are trying to eat soup with a pair of tweezers.
This card is, thus, an image of manic futility.

## Symbols associated with the card

✡ **Esoteric Title:** Lord of Unstable Effort

✡ **Astrology:** Moon in Aquarius

# Eight of Swords

## Keywords
IMPOSSIBLE CHOICES – LACK OF STAMINA –
FEAR OF MAKING THE WRONG CHOICE

## Divinatory meaning
A problem appears, or a decision has to be made, and you
are not sure what the right answer is. Often you are not in
control of the outcome as the responsibility for making
the choice is either out of your hands or will be made as
a group. Even so, you take on the whole responsibility for
the outcome yourself. You keep going over the problem in
your mind, over-analysing it, until it becomes
meaningless and you can no longer think clearly.
Recognise that the outcome is not your responsibility.

## Advice
Rest, and let others make the running for a while. Draw
another card from the deck to find a positive way through
your problem or what will happen when you tackle it.

# Concept of the card

To illustrate the Eight of Swords, the artist went over and over the
shape of the sword, putting layer over layer, resulting in a thick,
unreadable image. In the same way, if you go over and over a
problem in your mind, the result is sometimes neither clarity nor
a solution, but a sticky unclear mess from which you cannot
unglue your mind. The dominant colours in this image are grey,
green and pink, signifying disintegration, fear and weakened
force respectively.

## Symbols associated with the card

✿ **Esoteric Title:** Lord of Shortened Force

✿ **Astrology:** Jupiter in Gemini

# Nine of Swords

## Keywords
BAD DREAMS – MARTYRDOM – GUILT – DENIAL –
SELF-PUNISHMENT – OBSESSIVE BEHAVIOUR –
SELF-CONDEMNATION – SELF-VICTIMISATION –
NEGATIVE BEHAVIOUR PATTERNS – ADDICTION

## Divinatory meaning
You are anxious and worried about someone or
someone's criticism of you. This can literally lead to
sleepless nights, as you go over and over the situation in
your head. You feel guilt about the situation and are
blaming yourself. Your fears, although based in reality,
have been exaggerated out of all proportion. You have
laid on your shoulders total responsibility for the
problem, but this is actually an internal reaction to the
fact that the outcome of this situation is not in your
control.

## Advice
Once you have realised that the outcome is not in your
control and have recognised that there are others
involved, you can start moving towards a more positive
outlook. You can then assist both yourself and others in
finding a happier solution to your problem. Draw another
card from the deck to find a positive way through your
problem or to see what will happen when you tackle it.

# Concept of the card
The swords on this card loom out of the darkness, appearing as if
in a dream. Here the negative side of the swords is at its strongest,
for this is the card of nightmares and of the personality touching
a lesser death in sleep. The nine swords surround a dark image of
a hypodermic needle, representing addiction to negative
behaviour patterns and repeated mistakes. The writing on the card
is white, standing out clearly against the dark, just as the solution
to your problems stands out clearly to other people.

## Symbols associated with the card

✧ **Esoteric Title:** Lord of Despair and Cruelty

✧ **Astrology:** Mars in Gemini

# Ten of Swords

## Keywords
FEAR – DEPRESSION – HEART-BREAK – ANGER –
AGGRESSION – GOING OVER THE EDGE –
SPIRITUAL IMBALANCE – LOSS

## Divinatory meaning
This card heralds a personal calamity, stemming from a
loss. It may refer to a loss of material security, such as
losing a job or home, or to loss of emotional security,
such as losing a parent, lover or a friendship; or it may
refer to a loss of physical health. This loss has led you to
look deep into yourself, where all you see is a monster
and a complete failure. You start believing that your own
extreme criticisms of yourself are what others think of
you. It starts to affect how you communicate with others,
and in turn how they react to you. This sets up a vicious
circle leading to depression. The way to break out is to
realise that real monsters do not feel guilt.

## Advice
Recognise your faults and your greatest fears; examine
your worst nightmares, and construct their opposites. Be
aware that it is your own imagination making you happy
and unhappy. Recall something that makes you feel
happy, and experience that feeling for a while. Then,
remove the mental image making you feel happy, but
continue to maintain a feeling of happiness. This will
remind you that you create your own happy or sad
emotions. Draw another card from the deck to find a
positive way through your problem or to see what will
happen when you tackle it.

# Concept of the card

Ten sword symbols are shown on this card, each in various stages of
disintegration. They signify that you have lined these negatives in
front of you and built a wall with them. You are thus unable to see
the background of vivid clashing colours representing the energy
and joy of simply being alive. This image shows us that once you
have conquered your fears by recognising them, you are given a
great gift – the knowledge and wisdom to renew your life.

## Symbols associated with the card

✧ **Esoteric Title:** Lord of Ruin

✧ **Astrology:** Sun in Gemini

# Girl of swords

## Keywords
CONQUERING A NEGATIVE SELF-IMAGE –
REBELLION – POSITIVE – PRACTICAL –
CLEAR AND HONEST PROTEST – FEARLESSNESS –
COURAGE – REVELATION

## Divinatory meaning
Just a single word can break down years of self-doubt and
self-oppression. When this card appears you suddenly
gain inspiration and see the world around you, and how
you fit into it, differently. You gain the courage and
insight to fight for what you believe is just. There may be
a message, or new information, which sets you alight,
inspiring you to take up your mental sword to fight for
justice and change. You may become involved with the
law or find yourself battling against authority, but your
practicality and experience will lead you to take the right
professional advice. This card signifies mental victory
over the emotions.

People represented by the Girl of Swords are spirited
rebels (of whatever age) with the passion of the young for
a cause but the experience, practical organisation and
diplomacy of the mature. Together these allow them to
create the right environment for the changes they wish to
bring about.

## Advice
You are as old as you feel, and you have as much energy
as you want. Conquer your emotions; they are as unreal
as your ever-changing complexion.

# Concept of the card

This card represents a triumph over stagnation, brought about by
overcoming the fear of ageing. Within the myths and constructs
of our society, ageing is strongly linked to loss of beauty,
sexuality, virility, fertility and even intelligence. The media and
society pressure us all to conform in some way to these
paradigms. It expects us to take on roles defined by our ability to
conform outwardly to these ideals. The illustration on the card
shows, in the one image, the old self, which has been repressed
and constrained under years of self-doubt, physical restrictions
and a negative self-image. In the other image, a new, rebellious
energy burns away the old and stagnant self-image, turning it to
ashes. It reveals a new, crystal-clear vision of shimmering beauty,

as the ego becomes aware of the superficiality of these surface realities and confronts the inner self.

## Symbols associated with the card

✿ **Esoteric Titles:** Princess of the Rushing Winds – Lotus of the Palace of Air

✿ **Elements:** Earthy aspect of air

# Boy of Swords

## Keywords
CREATIVITY – LIMITLESS – THOUGHT – DEVELOPMENT – CLARIFICATION OF IDEAS – DEATH OF LIMITATION – ANGER – MENTAL STRUGGLE

## Divinatory meaning
With this card, events occur out of the blue and new people or new experiences come into your life. You can expect conflict to arise from the excitement, and a mental struggle to ensue.

People represented by the Boy of Swords are intellectuals who use their minds like weapons. They have rapier-like wit, and are able to cut through problems and people's feelings at one and the same time. Because their minds dart around so much, they have the freedom to see problems from every angle. Indeed, they can often argue ideas through from every side. This leads people to believe that they are aloof and have no real passion for or belief in what they say; as a result, they appear to be untrustworthy.

## Advice
If you put your mind to it, you can cut through old entanglements which have been tying you down, and thus pursue new goals with vigour. New ideas will come to you which may appear ahead of their time; but if you use your new mental skills humbly and with consideration, you will be able to convince others to follow you.

## Concept of the card

This card represents the direct connection between intuition and thought. The colours in this card have been reversed to represent the very different potentialities available; each Boy is a mirror image of the other. The Boy on the left is surrounded by a halo of strong pink energy. He is able to cut through problems that may seem insurmountable. His thoughts flow straight from his source of creative ideas, conducted through the staff he holds, to the muse on the right. It is this very speed of thought which leads the Boy of Swords to instability, for his mind darts around from one idea to the next. It is also thought without the goal of harvest, unlike the Man of Swords. Instead, the Boy is led by the green mist of his emotions welling up on his intuitive side. This is a volatile mixture and it can cause him to be quick to anger.

### Symbols associated with the card

✡ **Esoteric Title:** Prince of the Chariot of the Wind

✡ **Elements:** Airy aspect of air

# Woman of Swords

### Keywords
OPENNESS – HONESTY – DEATH OF PRETENCE –
LOSS OF ARTIFICE – FRESH INNOCENCE –
EMOTIONAL COUNSELLOR – CLARITY – OBJECTIVITY

### Divinatory meaning

This card represents an emotional loss, feeling alone and aloof from the crowd. You feel isolated from those you love. Traditionally, this is the card of the widow or widower. It has the consolation of clarity of thought and of being able to understand with a new wisdom, as well as being able to advise and console others.

People represented by the Woman of Swords are solitary, mature and thoughtful, able to see through the illusions of success and defeat to the core nature of a situation. Their judgment is keen, and the decisions they make, although hard, are just. The Woman of Swords is a good person to take advice from when you are in emotional turmoil.

### Advice

Cut yourself free from all old perceptions of who and what you are. Once you are thus freed, you will be open once again to feel happiness.

## Concept of the card

The Woman of Swords on this card is an elderly woman, her eyes are closed, and she is pensive and a little sad. She is enclosed by her own world of memories. She is dying, and thus the image is breaking up and is fuzzy, as if it is about to disappear. She represents a lifetime of experiences, many bitter and sad. Now she can look back on them, released from illusions of physical beauty, ambition and power. In her wisdom she recognises the masks we all wear as false protection; she is in the process of dissipating her own mask. She prefers to spend her days in the company of children, attracted by the one thing that is precious to her now, the bright shining life-force which makes their eyes shine like metallic balls and creates a halo of spiky light around their translucent skins.

### Symbols associated with the card

✡ **Esoteric Title:** Queen of the Thrones of Air

✡ **Elements:** Watery aspect of air

# Man of Swords

### Keywords
THE MIND – AMBITION – ENERGY – AGGRESSION – CONCENTRATION – EMOTIONAL CONNECTION – AUTHORITARIAN – FOCUS – DETERMINATION

### Divinatory meaning

The Man of Swords heralds a situation which calls for clear, direct thinking. It is about taking decisions without recourse to other people's wishes, thinking the unthinkable in order to achieve your aims and break free from a stagnant situation.

People represented by the Man of Sword are authoritarian, ambitious and wise. Knowledge is very important to them, for they believe that knowledge is power. They use it as a tool to mould the world for their purposes. They think quickly, and ideas come to them in a flash. They are able to take the wider view of a situation. Where others would draw back from an action, they take it forward without seeming to acknowledge the resulting pain inflicted on others. However, they are deeply emotionally connected, and their actions are always guided by a deep belief in justice and that what they do is for the greater good.

### Advice

Believe in yourself: you already know the solutions to your problems.

# Concept of the card

The energy of the Man of Swords is the energy of destruction and harvest. He breaks down energies into their simplest forms and then builds them anew. He is the creative aspect of the male, which destroys in order to transform. He rests on a throne, his legs bent as if about to spring up. Beside him, on a table, are placed the fruits of his destruction, his harvest, represented by corn and apples. The book on the table shows his thirst for knowledge, and the coins show that his destruction creates wealth.

The Man of Sword's power appears to come from clarity of thought and his rational male approach to problems. Yet the speed with which ideas come to him is a result of his strong connection to his female intuitive side. He is the male aspect of the Priestess, whose disembodied head with long flowing hair floats out from the haze of energy surrounding his head and dissolving into bees and light. It is her hand beside him holding the staff of love.

This paradox of male rationality fuelled by female intuition is indicated by the presence of two magpie glyphs on the top right hand corner. Magpies represent paradox. They are both black and white; they are solitary birds which group together and they build nests of great beauty by stealing bright objects.

## Symbols associated with the card

✿ **Esoteric Titles:** Lord of the Wind and the Breezes – Lord of the Spirits of Air

✿ **Elements:** Fiery aspect of air

# Ace of Discs

## Keywords
SUCCESS – MATERIAL AND SPIRITUAL TRIUMPH –
BEAUTY – HEALTH – PROSPERITY –
MATERIAL GROWTH

## Divinatory meaning
This card indicates success and beauty in the material
world. It may be a new job, a new project, a pay rise, a
new home, redecorating your home or buying a car. It
concerns money becoming available or being rewarded in
some way for hard work. Your body and soul are at one,
and you enjoy health, wealth and happiness.

## Advice
All wealth is relative, as is material success. Your gains at
this time may be immense or small, but they will bring
you equal happiness. Now is a time to forget your worries
and concentrate on how much you love being alive.

# Concept of the card

This card represents the joys of the spirit made manifest in the
material world, resulting in the beauty seen in physical things. *The
Garden of Terrestrial Delights* (Eden) admonishes us to focus on
the centre of the mandala, and rest our vision within the circles.
On each side of the trunk of the Tree of Life are a man and
woman, standing under its light and fruit. The combination of
circular forms and angular diamonds blends to create an image of
unity and growth. This card thus contains within it the
potentialities of the Garden of Eden.

# Two of Discs

### Keywords
CHANGE – TRANSFORMATION OF THE MATERIAL – LUCK – ACCEPTANCE OF THE TIDES OF CHANGE – BALANCING OPPOSITES – AWARENESS

### Divinatory meaning
This card holds within it the concept of juggling with material things. Around you is a sense of impermanence in respect of jobs and homes. You have to juggle your finances to keep from going into the red. The Two of Discs can also mean gambling with material things in order to take a chance. You may gain much more or lose it all; you may transform your savings into a new job or home. In the long term, this signifies having to make a change that will bring about what you need for your future.

### Advice
Become aware of the fact that, although financially things look grim at the moment, if you keep going good things will be just around the corner. The only constant in life is change. Draw another card from the deck to find a positive way through your problem or to see what will happen when you tackle it.

## Concept of the card

Duality in the material world is represented in this card by two stone blocks, each with a mandala carved on its surface. One stone is set higher than the other, as on a pair of scales. The two stones are placed in front of a real sand bar located between Orkney Island and the west coast of Ireland. You can only walk out to this sand bar twice a day, when the tide is out. A few hours later, the sand bar disappears under metres of sea water. The tide has moved in this way since before the people who live and work in this area can remember, and their lives revolve around these tidal patterns.

### Symbols associated with the card

✡ **Esoteric Title:** Lord of Harmonious Change

✡ **Astrology:** Jupiter in Capricorn

# Three of Discs

### Keywords
WORK – DUTY – DILIGENCE – ENDEAVOUR –
STEADY PROGRESS

### Divinatory meaning
This card represents total concentration on the work at
hand. It is hard work for a purpose, the results of which
will provide rewards and make life easier in the future. It
concerns working hard for an exam or on a project in
order to increase your skills and material happiness.

### Advice
Be thorough and love your work.

## Concept of the card

The corn is being harvested; the cycle of growth must be started
anew, with the ploughing and the sowing illustrating the cyclical
nature of work. Work is never 'done', so we find beauty and
pleasure in doing everything. A dog runs through the corn field
on the card. He is mankind's best friend, and thus represents
loyalty, duty and love. In the forefront of the image hover three
discs, fragmental Rosy Crosses. They represent the recognition of
true duty.

### Symbols associated with the card

✡ **Esoteric Title:** Lord of Material Works

✡ **Astrology:** Mars in Capricorn

# Four of Discs

## Keywords
SET YOUR OWN BOUNDARIES AND LIMITATIONS –
SECURITY – AVARICE

## Divinatory meaning
When this card appears in a reading, you have choices to
make. You have become attached to the security and
stability of material forms of comfort, perhaps too
attached. You might even seem miserly and status-
conscious. You are limited in your vision of what you can
do with your life and what you can give to others.

## Advice
When life is emotionally difficult, clinging on to material
things can help to provide the foundation and security
you need to help you stay stable. This card may also
indicate defining your wealth and status through buying
property. Your environment requires change, with either
more structure or more impulsiveness.

# Concept of the card

This card places the viewer on the hill overlooking the ancient
sacred site of the White Horse of Uffington. It has been dug deep
out of the chalk hills, and the four discs are duplicates of its eye.
The horse is a representation of the Celtic horse goddess Epona,
goddess of abundance and fertility. She is carved out of the land;
so too do the boundaries of the fields beyond delineate the way
mankind carves out and defines ownership and wealth with
boundaries. When you come down from the hill and into the
plains, you lose this overview as you enter the day-to-day reality
which limits your vision of the world.

## Symbols associated with the card

✡ **Esoteric Title:** Lord of Earthly Power

✡ **Astrology:** Sun in Capricorn

# Five of Discs

## Keywords
WORRIES – DOUBTS – FEELING TRAPPED

## Divinatory meaning
You feel powerless and trapped in a situation and cannot see the way forward; everything is coloured by your fear of being trapped. This puts strains on your relationships and you are unable to concentrate at work. These stresses all confirm your worst fears of being trapped by failure at work or in relationships. However, the real problem is often something which you have been afraid to admit to. In situations like this, other people can often understand your problems more clearly than you can. Find someone to talk to, confront the source of your fears, and solve the real problems.

## Advice
Communicate honestly and clearly with yourself and others. Push for open discussion of your problems and fears. Draw another card from the deck to find a positive way through your problem or to see what will happen when you tackle it.

# Concept of the card

The Five of Discs signifies worry and anxiety about being left behind, feeling left out in the cold. When you try to see your future it is as if you are standing in front of a door opening into a dark room. You are unable to see what is beyond this door, and in your mind you create great tragedies and fears of failure and mediocrity. The room, however, may well be full of treasures and adventures, which you have yet to imagine.

## Symbols associated with the card

✧ **Esoteric Title:** Lord of Material Trouble

✧ **Astrology:** Mercury in Taurus

# Six of Discs

## Keywords
INNER WEALTH TRANSMUTING INTO OUTER –
PLANNED RISKS – THE REALM OF OPPORTUNITY –
FORGING SUCCESS

## Divinatory meaning
The Six of Discs heralds a successful time for new
enterprises. Your dreams are fulfilled. It is a time to
visualise what your needs from the material world are.
Aim to fulfil your goals. Be sure of what you want and
be ready to take up new opportunities as they arise. Now
is a time to communicate your visions to others.

## Advice
Communicate your dreams and ideas to others; they will
be inspired and help you realise your dreams. First you
must inspire others with your ideas, then together you can
make your dreams come true.

# Concept of the card

This card depicts Wayland's Smithy, which is found deep in the
heart of the Vale of the White Horse in England. At its base, the
discs have transmuted into heart-shaped shields. Wayland's
Smithy was originally a mausoleum of Neolithic warrior-kings
and their families. Long after the people who built the tomb had
died, and its original use was no longer remembered, it still
retained its spiritual power. It was named Wayland's Smithy by the
Saxon invaders from Germany around AD 995. Wayland was a
Saxon smith god, like the Roman god Vulcan, and one of his
attributes was the forging of magical armour and swords, such as
Excalibur. Thus, the card shows the forge where magical swords
are made. These swords are the ideas which give you the power to
conquer the physical world and create your own Camelot. But
remember, you need your own Round Table of knights to help you
build it.

## Symbols associated with the card

✡ **Esoteric Title:** Lord of Material Success

✡ **Astrology:** Moon in Taurus

# Seven of Discs

## Keywords
FEAR OF FAILURE – YOUR FEARS OF FAILING ARE THE
ONLY THINGS PREVENTING SUCCESS –
REPEATED FAILURE DUE TO FEAR OF CHANGE OR
THE UNKNOWN – TAKE SUPPORT FROM OTHERS –
FEAR IS BY NATURE ILLUSORY

## Divinatory meaning
You have planned and thought out your dreams and
worked hard to start building them; you are now at the
stage when you become afraid of failing. You can only
see the obstacles in your way, and not the solutions to
your problem. Indeed, things appear to start going wrong,
as your negative expectations affect how you react. At the
root of this is your fear of being a failure, of being found
out. Ironically, fears often appear when you are about to
make the final breakthrough.

## Advice
To turn your situation around, you need to ask others for
help and moral support. Another person's point of view
can help you once more see the world in a positive way.
Face and accept your fears. Draw another card from the
deck to find a positive way through your problem or to
see what will happen when you tackle it.

# Concept of the card

On this card the earth has become barren and cold, and the discs
have become snowflakes falling on the frozen earth. This is the
wasteland of Arthurian legend, and it enjoins us to remember that
the land and the king are one. Because of the adultery of King
Arthur's wife Queen Guinevere with Sir Lancelot, the King lost
heart and faith; thus the lands of Camelot were ravaged by famine
and everlasting winter. So Arthur sent his knights out on a quest
to find the Grail in order to restore his lands, thinking that
salvation was to be found outside. The message of the Grail,
however, was that the land and the king are one. In other words,
your fears come from within, and, likewise, so does your
salvation.

## Symbols associated with the card

✿ **Esoteric Title:** Lord of Success Unfulfilled

✿ **Astrology:** Saturn in Taurus

# Eight of Discs

## Keywords
CAUTION – CARE – NOURISHMENT – PROTECTION –
INTELLECTUAL, MATERIAL AND SPIRITUAL GROWTH

## Divinatory meaning
You are in some way building on past experience and
knowledge, and are already aware of the possibilities
which this work can lead to – financial gain, a promotion
or being recognised for your skills. Whereas the Three of
Discs represents the beginning of study and learning a
skill, the Eight of Discs represents the mastery of a skill.
But you have not yet finished; the goal is in view, but not
yet attained.

## Advice
Be prudent and careful, making sure that you do not
slacken off and celebrate too early. Continue to work hard
and carefully. Give yourself the necessary time, space
and privacy to finish off your work.

# Concept of the card

This card illustrates how you have fertilised and ploughed the
land and then carefully sown the seeds for the next harvest. The
weather seems set to be fair and all seems to be going well as the
first shoots start to appear. The discs, which in earlier cards are
fragmentary and broken, are now becoming whole again. But
now is not the time to celebrate or to count your money; the
harvest is yet to come. Be prudent and wait as the green shoots
unfold, as their hidden possibilities become visible.

## Symbols associated with the card

✡ **Esoteric Title:** Lord of Prudence

✡ **Astrology:** Sun in Virgo

# Nine of Discs

### Keywords
SELF-AWARENESS – GAIN IN SHARING –
SUCCESS THROUGH SELF-FULFILMENT –
GROWTH THROUGH PARTNERSHIPS –
THE MORE YOU GIVE, THE MORE YOU RECEIVE

### Divinatory meaning
This card represents knowing that you have done the right thing. It is about being able to look back and see that what you have been and what you have created in the past was good. It represents a mature and evolved person, who knows that the greatest goal in life is to know oneself. The only way to do this is to experience life to the full, giving yourself fully to the task of living and fulfilling your talents. Doing this selfishly will not bring happiness – that comes from sharing your life lovingly with others.

### Advice
Give yourself fully, and with all your heart, to life. The more you give of yourself to living, the more you shall receive from life.

## Concept of the card

In this card sand, sea and sky meet. So too do body, mind and spirit; they are the trinity, the three work as one. The following story describes the way in which energies flow back and forth between our emotions, our actions and material situations.

A woman stands on the shoreline, picking out her worldly possessions from a small bag. She kisses each one as she throws it into the sea. A month later she returns, picking her way gently along the beach, stooping every now and again to pick up something she spots glistening in the sand. A century ago, when the land extended further out into the seas, a thief buried his hoard of coins here. The night before the woman returned to the shore, a storm had dug its way deep into the dunes, uncovering the coins in their flimsy canvas bag. The ocean gives as she receives, thus are the ebbs and flows of life.

### Symbols associated with the card

✡ **Esoteric Title:** Lord of Material Gain

✡ **Astrology:** Venus in Virgo

# Ten of Discs

### Keywords
EXTERNALISATION OF INNER WEALTH –
KNOWLEDGE – CREATIVITY –
PASS ON YOUR EXPERIENCE AND TALENT –
DO NOT HOARD

### Divinatory meaning
You have reached a stable, happy, secure and mature point in your life. You have what you need to be fulfilled emotionally, physically and spiritually. Now is the time to share it. This card represents close relationships, marriage, children and family. It also signifies the passing on of personal and family traditions or inheritance, be they monetary, genetic or emotional.

### Advice
Do not hoard this wealth to yourself; pass it on to others and enjoy the gifts you will receive in return. Recognise the inner gift you have been given, the ability to know and understand the complexity of existence. Share your knowledge with those who will go on after you.

## Concept of the card

In the background of this card is the woodland during springtime, sensuous and richly carpeted with a purple and green floating mist of bluebells. It represents the mysterious and transcendent beauty of nature, something we all take for granted. The discs on the card are represented by golden balls. These are the fruit of inner wealth and knowledge, the apple of knowledge eaten by Adam and Eve in the garden of Eden.

### Symbols associated with the card

✡ **Esoteric Title:** Lord of Wealth

✡ **Astrology:** Mercury in Virgo

# Girl of Discs

## Keywords
FERTILITY – CYCLIC RENEWAL – LIGHT-BEARING –
GROWTH – THE CHANGE FROM CHILD INTO ADULT –
EARTH TO EARTH AND ASHES TO ASHES –
LIFE CYCLES – PREGNANCY

## Divinatory meaning
This card represents the start of new growth. The seeds you
have sown mentally earlier in your life will begin to flower;
academic and menial work will be recognised. Your earlier
education and training will pay off, and you may receive a
message telling you of new projects or opportunities for
furthering your skills or education. The Girl of Discs can
also indicate that, as a parent, your children no longer need
you as when they were small; you are thus able to redefine
yourself as an individual again. This is also one of the cards
in the Tarot indicating pregnancy.

People represented by the Girl of Discs are quiet and
reflective. They have worked diligently and hard at
learning a skill or mental study and are now ready to
learn new lessons. Like a child growing into adulthood,
they have built the foundations and now have the
autonomy to develop themselves further.

## Advice
Immerse yourself in your present situation – it will
change and alter automatically and inevitably. Whatever
the new opportunities are, they will fulfil your needs and
allow you to become totally absorbed in your work.

# Concept of the card
This card depicts a voluptuous young woman lying down, like
Danaë, legs open to receive the caresses of a shower of discs. She
is the young, fertile ground in which the seeds of the future are
planted. In her body ideas and material wealth grow, flourish and
are born. Her body receives the acorn from which tall oaks grow.
She is channelling a ray of light. She is the fulfiller of tasks; she
is the annunciation.

## Symbols associated with the card

✿ **Esoteric Titles:** Princess of the Echoing Hills – Rose of the
Palace of Earth

✿ **Elements:** Earthy aspect of earth

# Boy of Discs

## Keywords
ORGANISATION – SOLIDITY – CONTINUAL RENEWAL –
STRUCTURE – DETERMINATION – PREPARATION –
PHYSICAL ENERGY – GRAVITY – TRUST – RICH REWARDS

## Divinatory meaning
You are about to come to a point in your life where you
will be rewarded for mental work. Money will appear as
a reward, and perhaps even a new job. The Boy of Discs
sometimes indicates travelling due to work, or being
given the chance to represent your company to others.

People represented by the Boy of Discs are diligent
and careful, able to use their intellectual capacities to
build solid foundations and create wealth. They plan their
work carefully and make good organisers. They can be
relied upon to give prompt and accurate information.
They are not concerned with being particularly
passionate or sensual lovers, but are reliable and
trustworthy and are likely to build secure material
foundations for family life.

## Advice
This card represents a time when your organisational
abilities come to the fore. Take the time to plan out your
next actions. In that way you will be more likely to gain
your goals.

# Concept of the card
The Boy on this card stands by the ghostly image of the stone-
carved mandala on the Ace of Discs. The mandala represents the
material forms and the earth. It is organic, showing the growth of
ideas. His mind builds up abstract thought forms which can then
be translated into physical reality, much like a designer or
architect. He is patient and careful, aware that detail is important,
but determined to build his dreams no matter how long it takes.
He understands the forces of growth and fertility on a mental
level, and would make a good planner of organisational
structures.

## Symbols associated with the card

✡ **Esoteric Title:** Prince of the Chariots of Earth

✡ **Elements:** Airy aspect of earth

# Woman of Discs

## Keywords
MATURITY – STAMINA – REPLENISHMENT –
FERTILITY – PHYSICAL BEAUTY – PROTECTION –
HEALING

## Divinatory meaning
You have been through a very hard period of your life, both emotionally and physically; now you are beginning to put back the pieces. It is important for you to feel rooted and safe for a while. You have found a comfortable home and job, and are happy once again in your surroundings. You have realised that further growth can only come through tending your inner garden and watching the flowers bloom. Psychologically, personal appearance and physical health are tied up together.

People represented by the Woman of Discs have an honest heart and are cheerful and warm; but they also have a serious and introverted side. This comes from their need to retreat occasionally to find the time to love and heal themselves. They enjoy surrounding others in a happy, creative atmosphere. They often have the capacity to heal people, both physically and emotionally, as they have learnt to heal themselves. They have built up their own security and are proud of their homes, which are warm and beautiful, although not overly materially rich.

## Advice
When you look in the mirror learn to see yourself as beautiful again. Then your physical health problems will be able to heal.

# Concept of the card

This card depics an older woman, representing maturity gained from hard experiences. She has travelled through a barren period of her life, and her physical health and appearance have suffered. Her image is broken up, representing stresses pulling her apart. But she is now slowly fixing herself together again; she is learning to take care of herself. That cigarette will soon be put out, and her scraped-back hair will be washed and combed free again. She is learning self-belief and self-love. As she puts back the pieces, she will look back and smile.

## Symbols associated with the card

✿ **Esoteric Title:** Queen of the Thrones of Earth

✿ **Elements:** Watery aspect of earth

# Man of Discs

## Keywords
SUCCESS – HEALTH – WEALTH – ADVISOR –
WORK – INTEGRITY – TIRELESS STRIVING –
REAP AS YOU SOW

## Divinatory meaning
This card represents a time of harvesting the fruits of
one's labours. However, this is not a time to relax or sit
back. Because your talents have been recognised, you are
being offered new opportunities; this will mean harder
work and even more responsibility, but it promises a
greater harvest than before. Remember that a life which
is all hard work and no play will sap your energies. As
you build up your foundations for the future, deals
involving property will go well.

People represented by the Man of Discs possess the
wisdom of common sense. They are loving and generous
when giving help and advice to others; and they love
improving other people's lives. Their authority is the
result of their hard work and acceptance of responsibility
for the harvest. Their energy is that of fertility, either
physical or material. They love the beauty of nature and
the security of the land. This love of beauty and security
causes them to plough their wealth back into adorning
themselves and their homes with beautiful objects and in
providing a secure foundation for their families.

## Advice
Occasionally allow yourself the time to meditate and
relax in the countryside. Get back to the source of your
powers by communing with nature.

# Concept of the card
The Man on this card stands surrounded by the contrasting
squares of material balance, in which there are hidden figures
representing action and work. He stands boldly and is obviously
a man, yet he wears robes and shoes. In our culture these are
associated with femininity, but in another time he would be a
sultan, a courtier, a Magus. It is through diligence, patience and
toil that he has been able to clothe himself in the apparel of
authority and wealth. Because he has gained his authority through
hard work and by using his talents to the full, he is content and
secure in his position. This solid foundation allows him to be
generous and giving. He allows his body to become a conductor
of fiery fertility. His harvest of material wealth also includes
physical health.

## Symbols associated with the card

✡ **Esoteric Titles:** Lord of the Wide and Fertile Land – King of the Spirits of Earth

✡ **Elements:** Fiery aspect of earth

# THE ATTIC

## The History of the Tarot Cards

◆

## Mystery

Because Tarot cards appear to be magical and profound instruments, people have long been curious about their origins and the reasons for their creation. Were they perhaps devised by some great mystic? Or maybe invented by a long-forgotten cult?

The answers to these questions are as tantalising as the question of how the cards themselves work. We simply don't know who created the cards; but this hasn't stopped a multitude of theories from being put forward over the centuries. In eighteenth-century France it was believed that they had been brought from Egypt by gypsies. At that point the cards were assimilated into the new occult theories by those wishing to exploit the need for a religion as libertarian as the politics of the French revolution. These occultists turned to the newly rediscovered antiquities of Egypt as their ancient source.

In the nineteenth century Tarot cards were thought to have been passed down by a secret Qabalistic magical sect – once again linking the cards to the period's beliefs about the origins of magical societies. In the twentieth century, academic scholarship has looked at the factual and historical basis of the cards' origins, revealing their continuous use for the game of *tarocchi* (first played in Northern Italy around the fourteenth and fifteenth centuries), rather than as a purely divinatory tool.

The history I have been describing is, nonetheless, a cohesive one: Tarot cards have at all times been all things to all people. Their method of use and the belief systems surrounding them are no different from any other field of human study. Philosophy, history and science have all changed according to the sensibilities and beliefs of each period; and so too, the cards fit into the mindset of each age.

The history of the cards is an interesting and controversial one. Historians are divided over the question of whether the cards were originally used for divination. The 'non-believers' camp is usually headed up by art historians and other academics, whilst the 'believers' camp tends to hold less rigidly academic views and comes from more varied backgrounds.

Of course, we all come to this question with our own preconceptions. Mine come from first using the cards as a teenager and finding – to my surprise – that they seemed to 'work'. I have no explanation for this. Later, I took two degrees in art history and learnt the pros and cons of the academic approach to the history of visual objects. I have continued to use the cards as a divinatory tool, and I continue to be interested in their history.

It should be clear from this description that my approach to the history of the cards will essentially be that of a believer. I have tried, where possible, to include the important texts from each period so that you can make up your own mind. The history of the Tarot cards shows that it is always difficult to define a final truth – especially where people's egos are involved in defining that truth. The cards become a tool for understanding the ever-changing, and yet essentially similar, beliefs and desires of people through the ages.

# From Playing Cards to Tarot Cards

We cannot look at the origin of the Tarot cards without looking at the origin of playing cards in general. The earliest come from China, where they were used before the year AD 1000. These cards were quite different from European cards, being made of long strips of paper printed with simple images and characters. There are a number of different types of decks. One included two cards with schematic images on them of a man and a woman, possibly the predecessors of the court cards of the European deck.

Colonies of Chinese were living in Iranian towns around the 1290s, and it seems probable that card games were taken up by local people and modified for their own use. This provided the pack with the court cards in the form of figures such as the Shah (King) and Vizier (Knight). Cards also seem to have migrated before 1300 to Mameluke, Egypt and Syria, possibly through Russia. It is likely that the game was brought to Italy by the Venetians whilst trading with the Saracens during or just before the 1370s. This started the amazingly rapid spread of playing cards throughout Europe. However, playing cards seem to have appeared in Switzerland and Italy at almost the same time: the earliest written sources mention the prohibition of playing cards at Bern in Switzerland in 1367 and in Florence in Italy in 1377. This indicates that the cards were common and that their use for gambling made them unpopular with the authorities.

It is believed that the Middle Eastern versions of the playing cards influenced the designs and form of the cards found in Italy. The earliest decks of playing cards are different from Tarot cards in that they comprise fifty-two cards instead of seventy-eight, they did not have the Major Arcana or 'trump' cards and they normally did not have queens. The first time queens are mentioned in a deck of cards is in 1423, when St Bernadine of Siena preached against the cards in the church of San Petronio in Bologna, mentioning a pack of fifty-six playing cards, and listing the queens. The rest of the cards were divided into four suits, more or less following the same numbering and names as those found in the

Tarot pack: cups, swords, coins and polo sticks. The latter were probably renamed as batons, because the game of polo was unknown in Italy. It is interesting to note that the suits of cards in Switzerland and Italy are now quite different, suggesting that either the original source of the cards was quite different for these two countries or that each culture saw the original images differently.

| Italy | Switzerland |
|-------|-------------|
| Sword | Shield |
| Baton | Acorn |
| Cup | Rose |
| Coin | Bell |

In Europe the existence of decks of fifty-two cards precedes the invention of the Tarot by around seventy years. The first written evidence for the Tarot cards dates from 1442, when an entry was made in the record books of the court at Ferrara, referring to *'Pare uno carte trionfi'*. Similar entries can also be found for the years 1452, 1454 and 1461. It is certain that these *trionfi* (or 'triumphs') were Tarot cards because a sermon on games by a Franciscan friar in Umbria in the late fifteenth century mentions the *trionfi* and lists the additional 'triumph' cards in order. The names and the order of these cards are similar to, but not quite the same as, a modern deck of Tarot cards.

| 15th-century *Trionfi* | Atavist Tarot |
|------------------------|---------------|
| 1. The Juggler | 1. The Magus (Juggler) |
| 2. The Empress | 2. The Priestess (The Papess) |
| 3. The Emperor | 3. The Empress |
| 4. The Papess | 4. The Emperor |
| 5. The Pope | 5. The Hierophant (The Pope) |
| 6. Temperance | 6. The Lovers (Love) |
| 7. Love | 7. The Chariot (The Triumphal Chariot) |
| 8. The Triumphal Chariot | 8. Adjustment (Justice) |
| 9. Fortitude | 9. The Hermit (The Hunchback) |
| 10. The Wheel | 10. Lust (Fortitude) |
| 11. The Hunchback | 11. Fortune (The Wheel) |
| 12. The Hanged Man | 12. The Hanged Man |
| 13. Death | 13. Death |
| 14. The Devil | 14. Art (Temperance) |
| 15. The Arrow | 15. The Devil |
| 16. The Star | 16. The Tower (The Arrow) |
| 17. The Moon | 17. The Star |
| 18. The Sun | 18. The Moon |
| 19. The Angel | 19. The Sun |
| 20. Justice | 20. The Aeon (The Angel) |
| 21. The World | 21. The Universe (The World) |
| 0. The Fool | 0. The Fool |

The earliest surviving Tarot is an incomplete hand-painted set, probably made in 1441 for the court of Filippo Maria Visconti, Duke of Milan. This is generally known as the *Visconti di Modrone* pack. This type of deck was expensive to make, being decorated with costly materials such as gold leaf, and so they were very much limited to use by courtiers. The expense and beauty of these cards is one explanation of why they have survived. However, it does not mean that they were either the first Tarot cards to be created or that cheaper, printed decks were not already being used by other levels of society at the time.

## Major Arcana

But why were the 'triumph' cards added? It seems likely that a game (such as bridge) was invented requiring the use of cards to triumph over other cards in the deck during the course of the game.

Petrarch's *Triumphs* certainly seem to be the most likely source of inspiration for the cards, as the original name of the cards *trionfi* indicates. The fact that the early painted cards were not numbered, and thus the players would have had to have known which card triumphed over which, suggests that the order would have been well-known to a casual observer. It was probably related to a recognisable and popular narrative.

By the early sixteenth century Tarot cards were not the only decks with images that could be arranged into a hierarchical sequence. The 1525 inventory of the contents of Alessandro di Francesco Rosselli's shop lists packs with such diverse names as *The game of our Lord and the Apostles, The game of Seven Virtues, The game of the Planets* and *The game of the Triumphs of Petrarch.*

The last pack is the most interesting. The Italian poet and scholar, Petrarch, wrote the story of the *Triumphs* sometime between 1340 and 1374. The narrative of the *Triumphs* follows the course of Petrarch's love for Laura, including her death from the plague in 1348 (when he wrote the *Triumph of Death*) up until the year of his own death in 1374 (when he wrote the *Triumph of Eternity*).

Because the narrative of the *Triumphs* is so close in relation to the subjects depicted on the Tarot cards, it has been believed to be the original source of the Tarot cards. It was certainly a popular source for allegory in Renaissance art. Images of the triumphs of love, time or death can be found in secular art – from wall-paintings and tapestries to linen-chests.

The story related in the poem of the *Triumphs* first introduces Cupid and his captives, including the Emperor and Empress; thus Love triumphs over, or conquers, all mortals. The second stanza of the poem introduces Chastity, who thus conquers Love. Death follows next, as he triumphs over both Love and Chastity. The Devil often appears in engravings of the Death stanza, as he is shown taking the sinners away to Hell, whilst an angel takes the saved to Heaven. Time comes next, and he triumphs over Death (time heals all) and illustrations of this stanza show a hunched figure similar to the figure of the Hermit. Then comes Fame, who triumphs over Time, and illustrations of this stanza are similar to the Chariot card. The last stanza shows Eternity, who triumphs over Fame. It is illustrated with the Sun and the Moon as its captives. The last stanza also has the four beasts of the World card walking ahead of the triumphal chariot. The four beasts are the angel, lion, ox and eagle from Revelations, identified with the four evangelists Matthew, Mark, Luke and John.

Although the allegorical images found in Petrarch's *Triumphs* are similar to the Major Arcana of the Tarot cards, they are not the same. Images of the Tower, the Star, the Hanged Man and the Papess do not appear in Petrarch's poem; and images of Fame and Chastity do not appear in the *trionfi* cards. So it seems that the *trionfi* probably had behind them a different narrative, similar to the idea of Petrarch's *Triumphs* but which had perhaps been adapted verbally and widely assimilated.

The renowned art historian, Gertrude Moakley, indicates that the Tarot cards might have been adapted from figures alluding to the *Triumphs* in carnival processions, thus explaining the existence of the Fool and the Juggler – the Juggler being the spirit of carnival, and the Fool, the last card, being the spirit of Lent, which follows after the carnival. She suggests that this kind of card game was the origin of modern *minchiate* cards found in Florence. The images on the *minchiate* cards are comparable to those found on Tarot cards, but are no more similar to the story of Petrarch's *Triumphs* than the *tarocchi* cards of the time. They are more likely to have been a later version of the earlier *trionfi*. Thus, they would have travelled down from the northern Italian courts, rather than be the source of the *trionfi* themselves.

## Minor Arcana

In the majority of the early decks, the cards of the Minor Arcana were illustrated with simple patterns made from the symbols of each of the suits, leaving less scope for symbolic interpretation. However, one of the earliest printed decks of *tarocchi*, the Sola-Busca deck from around 1470–90, has a much more complex rendering of the suit cards. For example, in this deck the Ten of Coins shows a chest of gold coins being opened by Cupid, who is either taking away or putting in another coin. Beside the chest is a guard dog and hanging off the lid of the chest is a peacock feather, a symbol of luxury. The Three of Swords shows a heart being pierced by the swords, probably representing a broken heart or grief. However, these cards are not traditional *trionfi*, as the trump cards mainly illustrate characters from Roman antiquity, largely Emperors and military figures, rather than the usual symbolic figures such as the Lovers or Justice.

So it seems probable that when the Italians first decided to vary the illustrations on the standard pack of playing cards they included many complex and varied interpretations of literary narratives and symbolic images. However, it is curious that all of the surviving early hand-painted decks lack the Tower and Devil cards. This is unlikely to be a coincidence: these two cards might have been seen as unlucky or blasphemous and were later removed from the deck, or perhaps the way in which they related to an original narrative behind the cards was too controversial. I believe that the decks would originally have had these cards, rather than have been made without them, as literary sources (such as sonnets published in Venice) describe the missing cards being used. It was not long, however, before the images became standardised (probably as the game of *trionfi* itself was standardised) but not completely bowdlerised, for some of the more controversial cards stayed.

## Literary uses of the cards

By the early sixteenth century the name given to the cards had changed to *tarocchi*. Unlike *trionfi,* this name described the deck as a whole and not just the cards of the Major Arcana. It is also at this time that literary sources (rediscovered by Kaplan) begin to illustrate how the cards could be used for purposes other than gaming. In 1534 an author by the name of Triolo Pomeran da Cittadela wrote a series of poems using the trump cards, or Major Arcana, to praise the renowned ladies of Venice. The work was titled *Triomphi de Triolo Pomeran da Cittadela: composti sopra Li Terrocchi in Laude delle famose Gentil donne di Vinegia.*

### Emperor
With profound wisdom, pure honesty and utmost courtesy
written on her forehead,
Benedetta Pisani teaches in this world
how to walk to heaven on the narrow path.
The *Emperor*, with his glorious and cheerful face,
leads this gentle lady by his side
to defend God's holy faith
against any who do not believe.

### Chariot
I will raise my voice, perfect my style,
as long as I sing the high praises of Love
For Maria Laureda, the gentle soul.
Unique on earth in beauty and valour,
her immortal fame, from the Ganges to Tyle,
shines bright with singular splendour,
she holds the *triumphal carriage*
as a sign of her proud, worthy state.

### Wheel
Like a red rose enfolding to the dawn sky
striking and lovely,
So Paula the Moor, even more charming and nimble,
uncovers the graceful features of her face.
Her manner of speech seems divine,

gentility surrounds her always.
With a merry face, she holds the *wheel*
that bodes uncertain hopes to the blind world.

### Temperance

There is so much virtue in her sacred looks
that everyone in the meadow would smile at her,
the beautiful Bianca Zena, in whose breast
chaste thoughts sojourn and flourish.
A *temperance* delightful to behold
adorns her face.
In her fine habits such as virtue has
could give salvation to all the world.

### Fire

The shores, the mountains, every hill would smile
and the sweet air would gently move the flower
as she appears, Bianca Contarina,
graceful, proud, shining brighter than the sun.
Her superior, most divine beauty
inflames and softens any obstinate mind.
Thus does the lovely lady hold the *fire*
that is love's net and virtue's pillar.

This is not a Tarot divination as we would recognise it today. Here the cards are picked by the five women and the poet then goes on to create a flattering poem about each woman using the symbolic meaning of each card and the perceived qualities of the woman.

This poem follows the literary practices of the day in which authors would use the rhetorical form known as *ekphrasis* to describe a painting, aiming to bring it vividly before the reader's mind. The poem combines this tradition with that used by Petrarch in his *Canzoniere* ('Song Book'), in which he used poetry to praise beautiful women (particularly his beloved Laura).

Paradoxically, this form of using the cards is closer to Tarot divination as it is practised today than to some later forms of divination. Here they are a tool for helping elucidate the personality and motives of the person who has picked the cards, rather than their eighteenth and nineteenth-century use simply as a method of predicting events that will occur in the future. Fortune telling of a more mundane type was practised at this time, in a form called Brevi. These were little mottoes describing events that would happen in the year ahead. These were written and then picked at random to be sent to people at the beginning of the New Year, usually as part of the entertainments for Twelfth Night.

An interesting parallel from more recent years is Italo Calvino's novel, *The Castle of Crossed Destinies*, which tells of a group of travellers stranded in a castle and struck dumb, who use the Visconti-Sforza deck of *tarocchi* to describe themselves and tell their various stories to their companions.

This is not the only example of such a use of Tarot cards. A poem published by G. Bertoni around 1550 also used the images on the Tarot cards to describe the virtues of the ladies of the court of Isabella d'Este. Likewise, Giambattista Susio wrote a poem in 1570 doing the same for ladies of the court at Pavia.

In 1527 an earlier set of such *tarocchi appropriati* (personalised Tarots), written in macaronic verse by Teofilo Folengo, was published in Venice. Macaronic verse is a humorous mixture of Latin and Italian, which mocks the self-importance of using Latin. The last verse describes a poet, Limeruno, telling his friend, Triperuno, how he was requested to compose four sonnets for four people (Giuberta, Focilla, Falcone and Mirtella) which he was commanded to recite before the Queen. When Limeruno arrived at the palace, the two men and two women led him into a room where the trump cards were dealt to each person in turn. Limeruno was then asked to compose the sonnets using the cards that had been dealt to them. Unlike Triolo Pomeran da Cittadela's set of sonnets, these poems reveal some similarities with Tarot divination as it is practised today, for the cards were apparently chosen at random for each person.

For the fate of Giuberta, the sonnet draws on Justice, Angel, Devil, Fire and Love.

> While the *Fire of Love* always burns in me,
> I bethink myself and say,
> It is not the *Angel* of God, but rather the Enemy,
> whom *Justice* expelled from heaven.
> Yet you adore him like an *Angel*,
> calling his *Flames* sweet intrigue,
> but I deny this, for never was there
> a friend of *Justice* who became so enamoured of the *Devil*.
> *Love* of woman is the ardour of a black spirit.
> If in his eyes he seem an *Angel*,
> let not his face deceive you, for it is fraud, not *Justice*.
> *Justice* it cannot be, when malice
> relives the crude archer of his torches,
> and *Satan* appears as an *Angel* of Light.

This could be a comment on a love affair which Giuberta has had. But it is also a comment on the nature of Love in general.

For Focilla, a prudent woman, Limeruno continues with World, Star, Wheel, Strength, Temperance and Juggler.

> This fortune in the *World* is like a *Juggler,*
> now raising someone, now bringing him down;
> there is no *Temperance* in it, rather it destroys
> the *Strength* of one who was born under a wicked *Star.*
> A *Temperate,* strong and beautiful woman
> whose splendour outshines the *Stars*

holds the unstable *Wheel* humble and low,
and playfully she to the *World* appeals.
*Temperately* she has always used her *Strength*
so as to lead the *World* and, with it
the fate-dealing *Stars* in jest.
Let *Fortune* with her lightness
go among the *Stars* with extreme powers,
he who knows to *Temper* himself keeps her
and the *World* in check.

This sonnet describes Focilla's qualities. But it also has political overtones, as it exhorts those with extreme powers to use their power temperately – otherwise fate, and presumably God's Justice, will bring them down.

The third sonnet is for Falcone. It relates that the Pope and the Emperor have the power to free the Europeans held under Turkish rule. The cards used are the Moon, Hanged Man, Pope, Emperor and Papess. The sonnet is couched in puzzling language and the poet's companion Triperuno remarks, 'In this sonnet you are often playing at being dumb.' This indicates that by playing the Fool, Limeruno is deliberately trying to obscure an overt political commentary.

The fourth sonnet, for Mirtella, uses Sun, Death, Time, Chariot, Empress and Fool.

What could be more *Foolish* under the *Sun,*
than to wait for a *Time* to enjoy time.
Death on the *Empress's Chariot,*
hastens to turn our children into dust.
Beneath the *Sun* the lad quickly arranges the violets on
    the *Chariot.*
Crazy is the person who fears the mortal arrow
which flies to kill even the *Empress.*
But *Fools* there will be on the Imperial *Chariot.*
Stay woman, while you are lovely
for the *Sun* ages and kills all beauty.
Enjoy, mad woman, enjoy the flowers while you can.
The *Chariot* flies with *Sun*, and as the cemetery fills.
The Black *Empress* grows more beautiful.

This poem appears to be more straightforward: Limeruno is telling Mirtella to enjoy life where she can, as death is never far away. The fleeting nature of beauty and the inevitable mortality of beautiful women was a common subject in poetry.

Limeruno then concludes that he would have composed the reading with less hastiness had the distribution of the cards been in his power. In order to make amends he offers a final sonnet where he says that the choice is entirely his, and he uses twenty-one of the twenty-two trumps, leaving out the Fool. It is likely that Limeruno himself was meant to represent the Fool.

*Love* under whose *Reign* many enterprises
are made in vain by *Time* and shattered by *Fortune*,
saw *Death* on the *Chariot*, horrendous and dark,
wending his way among the captives from the *World*.
By what *Justice*, said *Love*, have you never returned to us.
*Pope* or *Papess*,
*Death* unanswered, he who separated the *Sun* from the
    *Moon*
took away their defenses against my *Strength*,
and I know what that *Fire* is, said *Love*,
that seems now *Angel*, now *Demon*, and how one can
    become *Tempered*
Against it under my *Star*.
You, the *Empress*, hold sway over the body, but a heart
    that, though
*Suspended*, does not fall, has the renown of the *Sun*,
whose noble fame would tempt a *Juggler*.

Limeruno states that he used all the cards, but there appear to be eight cards missing. From this it seems that he has interpreted them within the framework of this poem, rather than used their names directly. He creates an interpreted meaning, which he uses to continue the story. Thus the Emperor = Reign, The Tower = Fire, Judgement = Angel, Time = Hunchback, Demon = Devil, Strength = Fortitude, Temperance = Tempered and the Hanged Man = Suspended.

We should not claim that this use of the cards was either commonplace, or even that it was true divination; instead, the poets would use the cards for a kind of free association. The cards let them demonstrate their virtuosity, and also allowed them to avoid any responsibility for what was being said: after all, they did not choose the cards. This is particularly the case in Folengo's sonnets, where the poet's ideas are politically controversial. Both sets of poems use only the triumph cards, or Major Arcana. This is probably because their imagery is deliberately symbolic, and easily translated into a literary description. They both suggest, but do not prove, that people were aware of a deeper meaning existing behind the images on the Tarot cards.

But these poems are not the only evidence we have from the sixteenth century of an understanding of the cards not directly related to their use as playing cards for the game of *tarocchi*. Italian historian Francesco Pratesi recently discovered two Italian lectures published in the sixteenth century, in which different meanings are ascribed to the Tarot trump cards and also to the sequence in which the cards appear. The variations in their interpretations indicate both that it did not take long for the original story behind the cards to disappear into obscurity and that, despite this, the authors clearly believed that the cards originally had a meaning.

# Use of the cards for divination in the Renaissance

Another manuscript, discovered by Pratesi in the same library, gives a clear account of the use of the cards as a divinatory tool. It lists thirty-five of the Tarot cards, including some of the suit and court cards, with the meaning of each card. It also includes a brief description of how to lay out the cards, showing that only thirty-five of the sixty-two cards of the Bolognese *tarocchi* deck were used. According to Pratesi, 'They are put down in five piles, making seven cards in each pile.' He then goes on to suggest that, like the method of dealing the cards found in Folengo's sonnets, each seven-card pile would be assigned to an individual and then read. The list of meanings is as follows:

| | | |
|---|---|---|
| Angel (Aeon) | = | wedding and settlement |
| World (Universe) | = | long journey |
| Sun | = | day |
| Moon | = | night |
| Star | = | gift |
| Devil | = | anger |
| Death | = | death |
| Traitor (Hanged Man) | = | betrayal |
| Old Man (Hermit) | = | an old man |
| Force (Lust) | = | violence |
| Temperance (Art) | = | time |
| Chariot | = | journey |
| Love | = | love |
| Baggattino (Magus) | = | married man |
| Matto (Fool) | = | madness |
| King of Swords | = | evil tongue |
| Ten of Swords | = | tears |
| Ace of Swords | = | letter |
| King of Batons | = | an unmarried gentleman |
| Queen of Batons | = | harlot |
| Knight of Batons | = | door-knocker |
| Fante (Page) of Batons | = | thought of the lady |
| Ace of Batons | = | annoyances |
| King of Cups | = | an old man |
| Queen of Cups | = | a married lady |
| Knight of Cups | = | a settlement |
| Fantesca (Maid) of Cups | = | the lady |
| Ten of Cups | = | roof tiles |
| Ace of Cups | = | the house |
| King of Coins | = | the man |
| Queen of Coins | = | truth |
| Knight of Coins | = | thought of the man |
| Fantesca (Maid) of Coins | = | young lady |
| Ten of Coins | = | money |
| Ace of Coins | = | table |

# Links with astrology

If the cards were being linked to divinatory meanings during the sixteenth century, there is evidence that as early as 1515 they were also being linked with astrology. Robert V. O'Neill, in his book *Tarot Symbolism*, published a woodcut made by the sixteenth-century artist Erhard Schoen, as an illustration for a nativity calendar, or astrological calendar, made for someone called Leonhard Reymann. God and the heavens are illustrated around the outside of the central panel. The central circular panel is then divided into a series of circles within circles. The innermost circle is illustrated with a landscape scene, probably representing the earth. The next circle surrounding this is divided into seven, and shows the seven planets known at that time. The next circle is divided into twelve, and shows the symbols of the twelve constellations.

However, it is the outermost ring that is most the interesting as far as the Tarot cards are concerned. This is divided into twelve panels in which the twelve houses of the horoscope are depicted, each one illustrated with images similar to those found in the Tarot cards. The first house shows a child being born, a concept which could relate this house to the Fool, or an undeveloped or childish man. The second house is illustrated with a scene similar to the Magician card, of a man sitting at a table dealing coins. The third house shows two mature women who could perhaps be related to the Papess and Empress cards. The fourth house shows a man ploughing a field, and is similar to a Chariot card. The fifth house shows two children playing, similar to the image on the Sun card. The sixth house shows someone lying in bed ill. The seventh house shows a man being married to a woman, and is similar to the card of the Lovers. The eighth house shows the figure of Death with his scythe. The ninth shows a Pope and the tenth house shows an Emperor. The eleventh house shows the Wheel of Fortune. The twelfth and last house shows a man in the stocks, an image similar to the Hanged Man.

From this woodcut it is possible to speculate that at least some of the images used in the cards relate to an astrologically-based narrative, with the World or Universe card at the centre. However, not all of the images used in this woodcut fit with the Tarot cards – for instance, Temperance, Strength and the Hermit are all missing from the print. So it may well be that instead of the Tarot images being influenced by images used in astrology, the designs created for the houses were influenced by the Tarot cards. Thus, at a time when the cards were beginning to be looked at as divinatory instruments, we find an artist connecting them with that age-old method of divination, astrology.

# Changes in card design in the Enlightenment

The card game of *tarocchi,* and its divinatory use, continued to spread rapidly throughout Europe from the sixteenth century onwards. And, as is inevitable in the course of travel and time, the designs on the cards changed. By the late eighteenth century their name had changed: they were now called Tarot cards, a French derivative from the Italian name of *tarocchi.* Not only the name of the decks changed, but also the names of the cards and some of the images on them. For instance during the French Revolution the Empress and Emperor cards were changed to the Grandmother and Grandfather.

The pack most commonly used at this time was the Marseille pack. Kaplan, in his *Encyclopedia of Tarot,* proposes that the Marseille type of pack first came from Italy. He refers to part of a pack of Tarot cards found in a well in the Sforza Castle, which bear some similarity to the Marseille cards. The Two of Coins has the following inscription written on it: 'PAVLINVS CASTELETO FECIT 1499' ('Paulinus Casteleto made me 1499'). Because of the date on the card found in the well, this type of deck may have been the original source of the early painted Italian Tarot cards.

Milan was occupied by the French at this time, and thus French soldiers may perhaps have taken home a pack similar to this after playing card games with the locals. Once it was in France, it could have been copied and slightly altered to make the classic Marseille-type pack.

Court de Gébelin's ideas were not far from other proposed histories which had already grown up around ordinary playing cards. An English journal, *The Ladies Magazine,* tells its readers of another popularly believed origin of the Tarot cards, one which was more influenced by French patriotism than by French occultism. It states that Tarot cards were invented in 1390 as a method of diverting the melancholic King Charles VI of France. This comes from a mistake whereby a deck of seventeen Tarot cards found in the Bibliothèque Nationale in Paris became known either as 'the Gringonneur' or 'Charles VI' Tarot. They were thought to have been those mentioned to Charles VI in the treasurer's account book, where a payment was recorded to a painter named Jacquemin Gringonneur 'for three packs of cards, gilt and coloured, and variously ornamented'. The date of the entry was in the year 1392. This identification and dating of the cards was accepted until 1848, when W.A. Chatto pointed out that they were Venetian in style, as was the dress of the figures depicted, and therefore probably made in Venice and thus should be dated around 1480.

There was a strong interest in the Tarot in France during the eighteenth century, and the cards were openly used for fortune-telling at the troubled French court. Some of the people involved in promulgating this particular use were closely involved with the occult mystical societies which had sprung up in France during that period.

Etteilla was one such figure. Etteilla was his stage name, which was created by a simple reversal of his real name, Alliette. He was a professional card-reader, and did much to popularise the use of Tarot cards for divination. In 1783 he published the third and final edition of his book *Etteilla, ou instructions sur l'art de tirer les cartes,* which explained how to use Tarot cards for divination and included an altered deck to be used for this purpose. In this edition he proposed that the Tarot cards were of Egyptian origin, and (using the images on the cards as hieroglyphs) stated that they were originally conceived of as an ancient book of wisdom, *The Book of Thoth.* (The Rosetta Stone was not deciphered until 1822, and the real meanings of the hieroglyphs were not yet understood.) He described that the book included an account of the creation of the world and the history of mankind.

Etteilla believed that the cards had been created by the mythical god/magician Hermes Trismegistus 171 years after the flood. Hermes Trismegistus (thrice great) was believed to be a real person who was both human and related to the mythical god Hermes in the form of prophet or seer. His written works, known as the *Corpus Hermeticum,* were believed to have been written before Plato. However, this dating appears to be erroneous, and they have been dated to after AD 100 from their textual style. His works related Egyptian and Greek mythologies and magic to each other.

# Changes in the sequence of the cards in the Enlightenment

The *Discorso* of Francesco Piscina (1565) comprises a short explanation of the order in which the cards are placed. This is in the form of a narrative, which from the Fool onwards relates to the state of humanity and then from the Death card explains the composition of the philosophical and religious spheres. For instance, the Popes and Emperors need the company of Fools and clowns for 'refreshing their spirits', and Love follows next with Justice because, according to Piscina, 'the leaders of the world, symbolised in the previous cards, must constantly avoid the passions'.

According to Pratesi, the other anonymous, and undated, *Discorso* found in the University Library at Bologna describes the Tarot cards in relation to ball games and chess as 'the best of them all since it is most similar to everyday life'. This indicates that the author saw the narrative told by the cards as an allegory of the state of man. He goes on to say that the swords and the staves are the masculine suits, and the cups and the coins the feminine. Then he praises the *trionfi,* or Major Arcana, which were 'added in order to remind us, with their beautiful images, of existing dangers and threats so that we can learn to avoid them'.

The author's interpretations of each of the Major Arcana cards are close to their current esoteric and divinatory meanings, for example:

> *Il Matto* (Fool) is examined alone. It is considered as the captain of all the 15 active triumphs. Its interpretation, connected with its role in playing, is that, contrary to every other defect, our Madness is with us during our entire life and cannot be avoided or transferred.
>
> *Il Bagattello* is seen as a Juggler: this card lets us see things in a favourable light, whereas they may not be so at all.

Etteilla also claimed that card-makers had, over the years, made a number of mistakes in their depiction of the images on the cards, declaring that he had found what the original images would have been. He illustrated these in his rectified version of *The Book of Thoth*. He also renumbered and reordered the cards to the following sequence:

1. Pope
2. Sun
3. Moon
4. Star
5. World
6. Empress
7. Emperor
8. Papess
9. Justice
10. Temperance
11. Fortitude
12. Hanged Man
13. Love
14. Devil
15. Mountebank
16. Judgement
17. Death
18. Hermit
19. Tower
20. Wheel of Fortune
21. Chariot
0. The Fool

This order followed the version of the narrative Etteilla believed lay behind the cards. Cards 1–7 represent the Creation of the World, whilst card 8 is the rest after the Creation.

Etteilla's description of the Egyptian origins of the cards seems to be traceable to a single source. An earlier account of the cards' Egyptian origins can be found in the writings of Antoine Court de Gébelin. He was a Protestant pastor, born in Switzerland at some point between 1719 and 1728 to exiled French parents. He returned to France after his parents' deaths and became closely involved with Freemasonry and Illuminism. In

1772 he began to publish the knowledge and beliefs surrounding these secret societies in a book called *Monde primitif,* eventually published in nine volumes over a period of thirteen years until his death in 1784. The work was scholarly in its content, and very influential; it was even subscribed to by the French royal family.

The basis of the book is the belief that there was an original civilisation or 'golden age', a utopia, advanced and, by current standards, perfect. Its disintegration formed the basis of later, less perfect, civilisations, but it might be attained once again by trying to rediscover its history and beliefs. Court de Gébelin tried to do this by examining the similarities in language and myths belonging to civilisations all over the world, whether still surviving or now extinct and surviving only in written accounts.

His examination of historical and linguistic sources was certainly not as rigorous as the procedures of modern linguistics and anthropology, two of the academic disciplines descended from this type of work. He tended to create links between different cultures based on his own intuition and the fact that words sounded like each other. For instance, he described the word *tarraux* (an old French spelling of Tarot) as being composed of two oriental words, *tar* and *rha rho*, which meant 'Royal Road'. However, he did not specify which oriental language he used and did not realise that the cards were originally called *trionfi* in Italy. He also went on to rename a number of the cards, claiming that the current names were the result of a mistake on the part of German card-makers, again without realising the earlier Italian origin of the cards. However, we must not dismiss his work too quickly: at the time, such intuitive leaps were seen as acceptable, and his book clearly reflects contemporary academic concerns.

Volume 8 of the *Monde primitif*, published in 1781, included an essay on the nature of the Tarot. Court de Gébelin explained how he visited the 'Comtesse d'H.', who had recently arrived in France from Germany. (She has been identified as Marie Helvétius.) He found her playing 'The game of Tarots'. They noticed how bizarre the images were, in particular the figure of the World:

> I take care to choose the one displaying the greatest number of figures, one which has no relation to its name: it is the World. I scrutinise them, and suddenly I recognise the allegory: and everyone abandons the game and comes to look at this marvellous pack of cards in which I have perceived what they have never seen. Each one shows me another of the cards: in a quarter of an hour the pack has been run through, explained, declared Egyptian; and since this is in no way the product of our imagination, but the effect of the deliberate and perceptible connections of this pack with everything that is known of Egyptian ideas, we promised ourselves one day to make it known to the public.

He went on to explain that the early sages must have put their ideas in playing card form, wisely knowing that such mundane items would hide their secrets from those who would wish to alter or destroy them, until such time as they were properly recognised again:

> It was time to rediscover the allegories which it had been destined to preserve, and to reveal that, among that wisest of people, everything, even including games, was based on allegory, and that those sages knew how to change the most useful knowledge into an amusement and make it into no more than a game.

He then described his understanding of the hidden meanings of the cards, illustrating them with a specially adapted version of the Marseille Tarot. This had been drawn by Mademoiselle Linote, a respected artist. He decided that the French word for the Juggler, *Pagad,* meant master and fortune, and thus described it as the Lord of Fortune dispensing man's fate. He saw the wand or staff held by the Magician as the wand of Jacob or the staff of the Magi. The Papess was renamed the High Priestess, and the Pope the Hierophant, taking the cards away from their original Christian context. In the same vein, he interpreted the Chariot as being the god Osiris triumphant, and renamed the Hermit the Sage. He also changed the name of the Hanged Man to Prudence, which together with Justice, Fortitude and Temperance completed the quartet of cardinal virtues. In order to do this he turned the Hanged Man card upside-down so that it appeared to show a man treading carefully rather than being hung by one foot. He identified the Devil with Typhon, the Greek version of Set, the enemy of Osiris. The Tower was renamed the Castle of Plutus. The Star was identified as Sirius, with seven planets surrounding it and Isis standing under the stars. The waters underneath the Moon were described by Court de Gébelin as being the Nile, guarded by two dogs, who represented the tropics. He also believed that the card-makers had made a mistake by naming the Judgement card after the Last Judgement, and indicated that he believed it represented instead the Creation. Finally, Court de Gébelin saw the World card as representing Time, with the four symbols in the corners representing the four seasons.

He then went on to state that the four suits were divided into the four estates, or classes, into which Egyptian society was divided. These are summarised by Decker, Depaulis and Dummett:

> Swords were the King and military nobility; Cups the priesthood; Batons those ocupied in agriculture; and Coins those engaged in commerce.

This division of the suit cards was also used at the time for reading fortunes with an ordinary deck of playing cards. One such description of the meanings of the cards comes from an issue of *The Ladies Magazine,* published in London in 1787:

By the four suits or colours, the inventor might design to represent the four states or classes of men in the kingdom. The *coeurs* or hearts denote the *gens de choer*, choirmen or ecclesiastics. The nobility or military parts of the kingdom are represented by the end points or lances and pikes, which through ignorance of the meaning of the figure we have called spades. By diamonds are designed the order of citizens, merchants and tradesmen. The *trefoil* or clover grass, commonly called clubs, alludes to the husbandmen and peasants.

The four kings are David, Alexander, Caesar and Charles, representing the four monarchies of the Jews, Greeks, Romans and Franks under Charlemagne. The Queens Argine (representing Regina, queen by descent), Esther, Judith and Pallas; which are typical of birth, piety, fortitude and wisdom. The knaves denoted servants to the knights; famous knights of the time were illustrated.

We can see from this that Court de Gébelin's ideas were not far from the mythology already surrounding ordinary playing cards.

# Links with mythology

Court de Gébelin also included an essay by another writer on the Tarot cards in the same volume of his *Monde primitif*. Louis-Raphaël-Lucrèce de Fayolle, Comte de Mellet, also claimed that the Egyptian origins of the cards were revealed to him during an innocuous meeting with the mysterious Madame Helvétius. De Mellet was perhaps a more significant writer on the meanings of the Tarot cards: it was he who first called them *The Book of Thoth*, and related them to the mystical writings of Hermes Trismegistus. He also related the cards of the Minor Arcana to a mystery story about the Ages of Man common in Greek and Roman mythology. Ovid, for example, tells of the Ages of Gold, Silver, Bronze and Iron in Book 1 of his *Metamorphoses*.

## The Golden Age

**XXI Universe:** This card has Isis in the centre and the four seasons of the year, represented by the four beasts, in the corners.

**XX The Angel:** This card represents the creation of man, with the winged figure blowing the trumpet representing Osiris and the droplets representing the tongues of fire by which the spirit of God animates dead matter.

**XIX The Sun:** This depicts the creation of the sun, with the two figures below representing the union of man and woman.

**XVIII The Moon:** This card represents the creation of the moon, with the terrestrial animals represented by the wolf and dog typifying wild and domesticated animals respectively.

**XVII The Star:** This represents the creation of the stars and fishes.

**XVI The Tower:** De Mellet calls this card the House of God and describes it as being the earthly paradise from which man and woman were expelled.

**XV The Devil:** This card represents Typhon, who comes to destroy the innocence of mankind and bring the Golden Age to a close.

## The Silver Age

**XIV Temperance:** The figure on this card represents the Angel of Temperance who has come to instruct man so that he can avoid that death to which he has so recently been condemned. She is depicted pouring water into wine to temper its potency.

**XIII Death:** This is simply seen as representing death.

**XII The Hanged Man:** He represents the accidents that befall man in human life. De Mellet connects this card with the prudence man must use when living in the world.

**XI Strength:** This card shows strength coming to the help of prudence and vanquishing the lion, which symbolises the wild and uncultivated land.

**X The Wheel of Fortune:** This card represents the injustices of fickle fortune.

**IX The Hermit:** He is the sage, who is searching for justice on the earth.

**VIII Justice:** This is the justice for which the sage is searching.

## The Iron Age

**VII The Chariot:** This card represents the crimes of the Iron Age and war.

**VI Love:** This card depicts a man hesitating between two female figures who represent vice and virtue. Thus, humanity is no longer guided by reason, but by base desire.

**V Jupiter:** This card replaces the Pope, and was found in the Besançon version of the Marseille Tarot pack. It represents the Everlasting mounted on his eagle.

**IV The Emperor:** This card simply shows a king.

**III The Empress:** This card correspondingly depicts a queen.

**II Juno:** The image of Juno with her peacock replaces the Papess in the Besançon pack. She represents the pride of the powerful.

**I The Mountebank:** He holds the rod of the Magi in order to deceive credulous people.

The final figure, the Fool, is unnumbered and represents madness, marching towards crime, impeded by a tiger snapping at his heels, who represents remorse. De Mellet also linked the last card with the Hebrew letter *tau* which he said 'signifies completion or perfection'. He later linked the other cards with the Hebrew alphabet, but in descending order rather than ascending, with the World taking the first letter, *aleph*.

Thus, the first forms of the occult or esoteric influences on the cards appeared in the eighteenth century, with Court de Gébelin providing an Egyptian origin and some links with the Hebrew lettering of the Qabalah. De Mellet went on to expound these theories in a more intelligible form. Etteilla popularised the use of the cards in fortune-telling and connected them with his other method of divination, astrology. They set the stage for the writers of the nineteenth century to pull the Tarot cards further into the burgeoning world of secret societies and the occult, and to make them a cornerstone of ritual magic.

# Links with magic

One of the most significant interpreters of the Tarot cards in the nineteenth century was Éliphas Lévi Zahed, whose real name was Alphonse-Louis Constant. This change of name gives a clue to his beliefs concerning the origins of the magical nature of the Tarot cards. He believed that the Jews were the primary source of magical teaching and that they had thus influenced the cards.

Although he enjoyed only a modest success during his lifetime, his writings became very influential in occult circles after his death, becoming the main source for what was to become the Western Mystery tradition. To summarise crudely, this was, and still is, a magical system whose sources are drawn from the mythologies of the West, especially those beginning to be synthesised in the magical practices of the Renaissance, although the original sources were far older and included the Qabalah, astrology, hermeticism and alchemy.

Unlike most of the Enlightenment writers we have encountered thus far, Lévi did not belong to any secret society or sect. Although he had been a Freemason at one point, it was not very long before he abandoned the lodge. He had no interest in selling his knowledge as a fortune-teller. Instead, his goal was to explain the ideas behind various magical practices and synthesise them into one tradition.

The Tarot cards were now well established as part of the magical tradition, and in contrast to Etteilla's tradition of fortune-telling, Lévi saw them as tools for magical meditation. Thus, he aimed at stripping away the later additions and returning to what he thought was the original form of the Tarot cards, the *Tarot de Marseille*.

# Links with the Qabalah

Last, and most important as far as the history of the occult in Tarot cards is concerned, Michael Dummet points out that Court de Gébelin, in an aside, linked the cards with the twenty-two letters of the Hebrew alphabet:

> The set of XXI or XXII trumps (Atous), the XXII letters
> of the Egyptian alphabet common to the Hebrews and the
> Orientals, which also served as numerals, are necessary
> in order to keep count of so many countries.

This is an example of where de Gébelin's knowledge falls down in the light of later understanding of Egyptian hieroglyphics: the Hebrew numerals and letters are not related to the Egyptian hieroglyphics.

Lévi moved the cards away from their supposed Egyptian origins, and associated them instead with the Qabalah. The Qabalah is a complex system of magical correspondences based around a mnemonic geometrical structure called the Tree of Life, which also uses the individual letters of the Hebrew alphabet and their meanings as part of its framework. The origins of the Qabalah have been traced back to Jewish mystics in Spain and the Languedoc in the late twelfth century. It began to become influential in Italy in 1486 when Giovanni Pico della Mirandola published the Hebrew esoterica, which had been translated for him by Samuel Ben Nissim Abulfaraj. Pico and other humanist scholars had an agenda to reconcile pagan mythologies and knowledge with Christian ideas.

The twenty-two letters of the Hebrew alphabet, as De Mellet had already shown, fitted with the twenty-two cards of the Major Arcana. Thus, it was in this way that Lévi associated the cards with the Qabalah and the Tree of Life. Dummett points out that true Jews would not have used representational images like the Tarot to hold their wisdom, as they were forbidden from using 'graven images' by the Second Commandment. However, if the cards were originally devised by a Christian with the same aims as Pico, they would not have felt the same prohibition.

There is no proof, however, that the Tarot cards were directly linked with the Qabalah at the time of their creation. Intellectually, however, when working with both the Qabalah and the Tarot images together they seem to create remarkably strong correspondences, linking, as they do, words, images and numbers.

Despite this, the way in which the Qabalah works with the cards was not immediately discernible. For example, De Mellet ordered the cards with the Hebrew letters descending from the World to the Fool, while Lévi placed them the other way round, with the Magus as *aleph* at the beginning, and the World as the last letter, *tau*.

Lévi also linked the suit signs to the tetragrammaton, the Hebrew for the name of God, יהוה, or *yod he vau he*, as well as with other occult symbols. This is set out in the following table, taken from *A Wicked Pack of Cards*.

| Suit signs | Cherub and Sphinx | Zodiac | Element | Alchemical Essences | Divine Name |
|------------|-------------------|--------|---------|---------------------|-------------|
| Batons | lion | Leo | fire | sulphur | *yod* |
| Cups | man | Aquarius | water | mercury | *he* |
| Swords | eagle | Scorpio | air | azoth[1] | *vau* |
| Coins | bull | Taurus | earth | salt | *he* |

[1]The alchemical essence azoth is the spiritual or higher form of mercury, believed by alchemists to be the first principle of all metals.

One of Lévi's students, Jean-Baptiste Pitouis, who wrote under the pseudonym of Paul Christian, went on to expand the circle of correspondences with Tarot by creating a complex system of links between the planets and astrology. He used the symbol of the Rosy Cross of the Rosicrucians to create a visual pattern for these links, publishing it in his book *Le Homme rouge des Tuileries* in 1863.

He also published a text which he presented as a rediscovered ancient Egyptian manuscript, describing an initiation into the mysteries of the temple at Memphis. This took place in a great circle made of seventy-eight gold leaves, on which were depicted images clearly related to those found in the Tarot cards. Despite the fact that this document was clearly written by Christian himself, it profoundly influenced the initiation ceremonies of many of the occult lodges of that time.

However, it was not until 1889 that Lévi's work on the Tarot resulted in the publication of a Tarot deck with images and an ordering related to his beliefs. It was published by the Marquis Stanislaus de Guita and Oswald Wirth. This couple were also involved with Dr Gerard Encauss, who had founded the Order of the Rosy Cross in Paris with De Guita in 1888. This lodge was to become one of the most important of the new secret societies blossoming in France at that time.

# Links with gypsies

It was also in 1889 that Dr Gerard Encauss published his influential book, *The Tarot of the Bohemians*, under the pen name Papus. Wirth contributed a chapter on astrology to this book as well as the designs of the Major Arcana cards. The of title the book recalls another cultural link often made with the Tarot cards and the bohemians or gypsies, who were renowned for their fortune-telling abilities.

We first find the connection between the gypsies and Tarot cards in a book called *Les Rômes, Histoire vraie des vrais Bohémiens*, published in 1857. It was written by Jean-Alexandre Vaillant, who was an enthusiastic historian of the gypsies. In this book he tells of a meeting in 1837 with a gypsy woman who was playing with a Tarot deck. However, from Vaillant's description of the cards she was using, it seems that it was not a Tarot deck, but a later card game called Trappola. Vaillant claimed that the Tarot cards were a holy book for the gypsies, and he described how they fitted into a mystical religion linked with Indian, Egyptian, Hebrew and Phoenician mysticism and astronomy.

However, gypsies are now believed not to have used Tarot cards for fortune-telling until the later nineteenth century. Up to this time their fortune-telling speciality was palmistry and occasionally divining using ordinary playing cards. The myth created by Vaillant (and repeated by Lévi in his *Histoire de la Magie* of 1880) became so firmly linked with their mythology that the gypsies took the cards on as part of the mystical paraphernalia that had been attributed to them.

Papus's book, *The Tarot of the Bohemians*, seems to have been inspired by his unrest with the growing scientific view of the world and the way in which it divided academic thought into increasingly distinct disciplines. He was hoping to use the cards to draw the disciplines together again, using art and science to understand religion, and, in the same spirit as De Gébelin, extract the underlying truths which appear to be at the root of most cultures.

# Use with the Order of the Golden Dawn

Papus followed Lévi's interpretations of the cards, adding his own creation of 'the cosmic wheel', a form of glyph drawn from numerology, the tetragrammaton and astrology. He then used combinations of these correspondences to interpret the cards. His system is very complex and became influential in later occult circles such as the Golden Dawn.

The Hermetic Order of the Golden Dawn was founded in England on 1 March 1888. It drew into its circle a group of people whose writing and designs for Tarot cards were to form the basis of the occult understanding of Tarot cards for the whole of the twentieth century

Their interpretations of the images on the Tarot cards formed a vital part of the Knowledge papers used by the order for teaching initiates. The images on the cards were firmly part of the whole group of occult correspondences used as meditative devices, from which initiates could gain insight as they travelled through the different paths and spheres on the Tree of Life.

The Golden Dawn interest in Tarot seems to have been influenced by Kenneth Mackenzie, a member of the Societas Rosicruciana in Anglia, which was founded in 1866. Mackenzie, who had discussed the Tarot with Lévi when he was in England in 1854 and 1861, was an important influence on Dr William Wynn Westcott. Westcott was anxious to create an esoteric group that would admit women as well as men (almost half of the members of the Golden Dawn were women) and which followed the Western magical tradition so strong in France and Germany.

Westcott wanted to provide an alternative to Madame Blavatsky's more oriental-influenced Theosophic Society. The French nineteenth-century understanding of the occult significance of the Tarot cards was certainly very influential on the Golden Dawn. Éliphas Lévi's works were translated into English in 1896 by another member of the Golden Dawn, Arthur Edward Waite, who had already translated Papus's *The Tarot of the Bohemians* into English in 1892.

Paul Foster Case continued the tradition of the Golden Dawn in Chicago, later founding his own group in Los Angeles, the Builders Of The Adytum (otherwise known by the abbreviation BOTA). His book, *The Tarot,* was published in 1927, and in 1931 he published a deck based on the Rider–Waite deck. This deck only used the outline of the images, allowing students to colour them in using a personal colour scheme based on their own insights. This more personal and psychological approach to the cards was also continued in Case's book, where he started to look at symbolism and meanings of the deck using insights from the writings of Jung and Freud. This psychological interpretation of the cards was later to make a great impact on the divinatory meanings given to the cards.

It was not only the Golden Dawn who influenced Tarot cards in America. In 1928 Manly Palmer Hall wrote about the Tarot in his great work *An Encyclopedic Outline of Masonic, Hermetic, Qabalistic and Rosicrucian Symbolical Philosophy*. In this book he brought an academic and encyclopedic approach to the understanding of the Tarot cards. In 1929 he published a new Tarot deck, created by the artist J. Augustus Knapp and which followed Oswald Wirth's rectified version of the Marseille Tarot.

Another Golden Dawn initiate influential in America was Israel Regardie, who had also once been a follower of Aleister Crowley. He made a great impact in American occult circles when he published his personal copy of the Golden Dawn's Knowledge papers in a four volume set. Then, in 1977 he published a Tarot deck which closely recreated the Golden Dawn's master set. The designs were drawn up by Robert Wang, who went on to publish his own influential book, *The Quabalistic Tarot* in 1983.

The Golden Dawn, however, did not last very long before it split into different factions, with Waite taking control of the society in 1903. By 1914 he dissolved his part of the order, going on to found The Fellowship of the True Rosy Cross in 1916.

# Creation of the Rider–Waite Tarot

Despite the Golden Dawn's short and tempestuous life, or maybe because of it, various members of the factions involved went on to create the theories which were to underpin most of the twentieth-century occult understanding of the Tarot cards. Waite published his own book, *A Pictorial Key to the Tarot,* in 1910, along with a deck of Tarot cards drawn by Pamela Colman-Smith, an American artist. This deck and book were published by Rider and Company, and came to be known as the Rider–Waite Tarot.

Waite and Colman-Smith's deck incorporated the Golden Dawn's systems of attributions, using alchemy, astrology, the Qabalah and the idea of fusion of male and female polarities. But despite the influence of Papus and Lévi, Waite denounced the Egyptian origins of the Tarot cards, and instead pointed out that the Tarot seemed to have no history before the fourteenth century.

This debunking of the 'false' occult accumulations around the Tarot cards influenced the design of Waite's cards. The images are not so esoteric that their meanings are hidden; instead of using openly Qabalist and Egyptian symbology (like the earlier eighteenth- and nineteenth-century decks), the designs on the Waite and Colman-Smith deck look like illustrations for a fourteenth-century storybook interpreted in the style of the early twentieth century. It is no coincidence that Pamela Colman-Smith used an image of a heart pierced by three swords for the Three of Swords in the Rider–Waite deck. It is believed that, in order to create a new Minor Arcana with pictorial symbols, she researched older decks. The Sola-Busca deck was a significant inspiration for her own designs.

These cards are perfect for beginners as well as expert Tarot readers, as their story-like imagery provides clues that can be easily read. The symbology hidden in the images, however, such as butterflies on the throne of the King of Wands symbolising Psyche or the spirit, provide a wealth of clues for the more advanced reader. This accessibility and depth is one of the reasons why the Waite and Colman-Smith deck went on to be one of the most influential and popular decks for fortune-telling in the twentieth century. Another reason for their success was Pamela Colman-Smith's innovation of creating individual designs for each of the Minor Arcana cards as well as the Major Arcana, making the Minor Arcana much more accessible for divining than they had been before.

# Aleister Crowley

By now MacGregor Mathers, the first leader of the Golden Dawn, had moved to Paris. In 1898 he initiated Aleister Crowley into the Outer Order of the Golden Dawn, and later, despite protestations from other sides of the society, into the Inner Order. Aleister Crowley was a maverick in occult circles at the time, openly espousing his particular form of 'sexmagick' and courting notoriety in the newspapers of the time. He was certainly too dynamic and unpredictable a character to stay under the wing of MacGregor Mathers for long, and so, by 1907, he had formed his own group.

Sometime around 1938 Crowley created his own Tarot deck called *The Book of Thoth*. The designs for this deck were drawn by Lady Frieda Harris in a futurist style. Crowley's book for the deck, also called *The Book of Thoth*, was first published with the help of Major Grady L. McMurtry in 1944. Crowley died in 1947, and it was not until 1969 that the deck of cards and Crowley's book were published widely.

The original illustrations for this deck are kept in the Warburg Institute in London, and show just how innovative Lady Frieda Harris was in her creation. With Crowley, she had begun to create a deck based on the early Italian Tarot cards, just as Waite and Colman-Smith had done. However, under the guidance of Crowley, Lady Harris, who was herself an Egyptologist, created a deck which was visionary in its concept. It drew upon the esoteric traditions of many ancient cultures as well as Crowley's own visionary fusion of Post-Newtonian scientific theories (drawn mostly from J.W.N. Sullivan's book *The Bases of Modern Science*) and magic. Although Lady Harris' designs are not as accessible as Pamela Colman's, the cards produce immediate intellectual and emotional responses from the reader at a much deeper psychological level.

## Celtic link

Another line of enquiry into the origins of the Tarot developed in 1920 when Jesse L. Weston linked the Tarot suits with the four Grail Hallows and the Celtic treasures of Ireland in her book *From Ritual to Romance*. The cups were linked with the Grail and the Cauldron of Dagda; the swords were linked with the sword of King David and the sword of Nuada, King of the Irish Celts (a precursor to King Arthur's sword, Excalibur); the wands were linked with the lance of St Longinus (which pierced Christ's side on the cross) and the spear of the god Lugh; and the pentacles were linked with the platter from which Christ ate the Pascal lamb, and the stone of Fal. Whether or not there is any truth to these Celtic treasures influencing the way in which the original suit symbols on playing cards were seen by the Italians cannot be proven, but the theory is an interesting one, especially in the light of the fact that the legends of King Arthur were popular in romance novels at the time, and inspired many wall paintings in Italian palaces.

# Current interest in the Tarot

Despite the continuing development of the Tarot by Crowley, Case, Regardie and others, interest in the Tarot cards suffered a setback in both Britain and America with the outbreak of the Second World War. Indeed, as Gareth Knight notes:

> At the time I wrote *A Practical Guide to Qabalistic Symbolism* in the early 1960s, it was very difficult to find a pack of tarot cards. Even the Marseille pack was not to be found unless one travelled to the appropriate part of Europe where the game was still played. And A. E. Waite's *Key to the Tarot* as well as the works of Regardie and Crowley and others were rarities on the second-hand book market.

This all changed at the beginning of the seventies, with Crowley's pack being published widely for the first time in 1969. I suspect that a major influence on the popularity of the Tarot cards was the 1973 James Bond film *Live and Let Die*, in which the Fergus Hall Tarot is used by James Bond to ensnare a voodoo priestess. Ever since then the number of books to be found on the subject, and indeed the many and different types of Tarot decks which have been published, has been growing steadily, as a trip to any book shop will prove. Kaplan's three-volume encyclopedia on Tarot cards gives plenty of examples of late twentieth-century Tarot decks for the interested reader both to examine and choose from.

I will not attempt a critique of the different cards and books produced since then, not only because of lack of space, but because we are probably too close to view them with any measure of objectivity at present. My only comment is that what lies behind this variety of different approaches to the cards shows us not only the strength of interest in the Tarot cards, but also tells us something about the individual nature of the search for belief in the later part of the twentieth century and the beginning of the twenty-first.

In conclusion, it seems clear from the history of the Tarot cards that there are two continuous and consistent trends. The first is the belief that the cards have the power to tell some hidden story, which, rather like a philosopher's stone, would allow us to hold great power if only we could understand. The second is that the way that hidden story is approached is, like every other aspect in human lives, always changing. It is not for us to judge the past as wrong or right, but to try to understand it; and if that understanding sheds light on our own beliefs, so much the better.

# THE KITCHEN

## Genesis of the Atavist Tarot Deck and Text

◆

## Sally Annett – the artist

### The Tarot deck

My Tarot deck is the culmination of more than eight years' work. I first began to produce images as potential designs for Tarot cards because of my desire to work within the figurative, symbolist, art-historical tradition. These images were not an attempt to produce a definitive Tarot deck, but instead a reinterpretation of the cards from a visual and aesthetic viewpoint.

My interest in Tarot developed during my final year at Bretton Hall, when I consciously started to develop a personal visual language encoded within my art work. The Tarot deck is ideal to work with as it embraces a plethora of symbols from diverse civilisations: Chinese, Egyptian, Christian, Greek, Indian and Celtic. It also provides an immense variety of condensed archetypal imagery, and a wealth of multi-cultural references.

My work, however, remains simply a personal, visual interpretation of the ideas held within the cards. I am searching for the One Truth, the marriage of science and religion. I am exploring ideas of Atlantis and the Apocalypse; I am examining pre-Christian epochs; I am delving into concepts from Plato to quantum physics, from astrology to Darwinism. I am looking for the roots of language and I seek out the archetypal in visual forms. So much has been hidden and forgotten. As such, this Tarot deck represents my personal quest for the truth.

The deck comprises many different artistic techniques. The Major Arcana, like the stories that go alongside the images, are complete elements. They take you on a journey, full circle. Their twenty-two images are painted in acrylics, glazes, wax and collage on five feet by three feet canvas and calico.

Next come the court cards. Most of these cards have been constructed from an original painting – except the Boy and Girl cards and the Queen of Wands where the original image has been duplicated and altered, representing aspects of the personality in development and remembrance. The Boy of Discs also has the Ace of Discs as a composite image within it, reflecting the physical presence of the suit. The manipulating and tampering with the images has been done either by hand or using computer-generated imagery. The photograph used in the Man of Cups is used by kind permission of David Legge.

Lastly, the suit cards, numbered one to ten, are created from my own paintings, drawings, etchings, collographs, photographs and sculptures. These have been scanned into the computer and woven, dropped and blended repeatedly, to create cards that steal and amalgamate from everywhere.

I use mandalas as frames and backgrounds throughout my pictures, drawing the viewer deeper and deeper into the card. I also pepper my paintings with glyphs, which are keys for larger magical concepts. Some of the more frequent animal glyphs I use are fish and magpies. In order to avoid putting the figures on the cards into a social or historical context, which would happen were I to use obvious gender or clothing signals, I paint them as stick people.

I owe an enormous debt to Lady Frieda Harris' Thoth deck and to the writings of Gerd Zeigler, as well as to Katherine Jameson, the painter who started me on my quest. Much of my work has been produced intuitively. Rowena Shepherd and I have worked in isolation, sending packages to each other to examine, correct and return. This was because it was important to me that her work was based on her immediate interpretations of my work rather than being directly guided by me. This has meant that the whole project has taken on a life of its own, surprising and intriguing to us both. Above all, the project has been completed with much laughter and joy; the Tarot is a pleasure to work with.

# Atavism

Many academic disciplines including astronomy, geophysics, pathology, genetics, anthropology and comparative religion, provide us with evidence of an older understanding of the universe. There are echoes of this in the transcripts of the world's diverse cultures, handed down through the generations; we find evidence of these in the scriptures of the world's religions; and even older stories survive, translated into the myths of different cultures. The oldest of these ideas are set in rock and carved in stone in hieroglyphs and cave paintings. They contain the ever-repeating archetypes of the sun, moon, stars, animals, men and women. They remind me of Venn diagrams showing interconnecting and interdependent ecosystems.

Indeed, the word 'translation' contains within it the notion of change; similarly, the word 'interpretation' has connotations of bias from one set of linguistic values to another. There are countless reasons to suggest that our global written histories are just not old enough to be accurate or specific enough in their information about our distant ancestors. In a letter from Alfred the Great to Bishop Woefero of Worcester in AD 895 concerning the translation of Pope Gregory the Great's AD 577 *Cura Pastoralis* into old English from the Latin, the way in which histories become lost is clearly illustrated.

> ... so completely overfallen is learning in England, that
> there are very few, beyond the Humber who have a true
> understanding of their divine services in English or can
> translate even a letter into English; and I think not on this
> side of the Humber either ... When I remember too how I
> saw, before it was all ravaged and burnt, how the
> churches of England were full of books and treasures ...
> it is as if they had said 'our forefathers who had these
> places before us loved wisdom ... their track may still be
> seen here but we do not know how to follow it' ... They
> did not believe that men should ever be so careless and
> teaching fall away so; they neglected their teaching
> deliberately intending that there should be more wisdom
> in the land, the more languages we knew ... then I
> remembered how the law was first founded in the
> Hebrew language, afterwards, when the Greeks learned it
> and turned it through skilled translators into their own
> language and also other books. Similarly, the Romans
> learned it, turned it through skilled translators into their
> own tongue ... all other Christian people have changed
> some part of it into their own language.

Alfred's letter was written seven centuries before the dissolution of the monasteries by Henry VIII, after which contemporary historians suggest that only two per cent of existing British religious texts, icons and relics survived. Some, like the monoliths in churches such as the eleventh-century building in Llantwit Major (South Wales), are carved with a runic inscription which remains undeciphered today.

Throughout Northern Europe there are ancient stones, cairns and burial sites, whose circle and spiral designs match closely with Australian Aboriginal dream-time patterns as well as with African and Mayan images. Sites of gigantic structures, tombs, pyramids and temples can be found across the globe. Archaeology and scientific examination of objects from these ancient cultures provide more and more evidence of sophisticated civilisations and of the trade and intermarriage between them. Religious texts talk of tens of thousands of generations past – their migrations and the changes and cataclysms they endured. Ancient Greek scholars openly acknowledged different nations' gods as aspects of their own with different names.

Common sense therefore leads us to believe that we have a common ancestry. We are but one race constantly evolving, critically linked to our environment. We all have only one source, both scientifically and spiritually.

This leads us back to the paradox of the Garden of Eden. The power given to us in the apple was knowledge and understanding of all things; in return we were thrown out of our paradise of innocence. In the new world God gave us the gift of free will, and thus, individual responsibility. This gift means that it is in our power to return to Eden if we so wish. However, history and conditioning block our perceptions and our understanding of the world around us. The free will we were given makes us create individual identities. This separation is the very thing preventing us from returning to our former blissful existence in paradise. Thus, as well as being aware of our individual identities, we should also be aware of the similarities of our lost joint histories, and not just the differences and barriers we put between us. We may have fought long and deadly wars amongst our different tribes, but in the beginning and forever, we are all part of the one human race.

# The 'lost' female histories

A woman clothed with the sun travailleth.
The great red dragon is cast out of heaven.

This verse from Revelations confirms that the female histories and knowledge are among the biggest casualties of the disappearing histories. The following extract, taken from the visions of Saint John, found in the Bible in Revelations, Chapter Twelve, contains a confusion of powerful female archtypal images left unexplained:

And there appeared a great wonder in heaven; a woman clothed with the sun, and the moon under her feet, and upon her head a crown of twelve stars: And she, being with child, cried out, travailing in birth, and pained to be delivered. And there appeared another wonder in heaven; and behold a great red dragon, having seven heads and ten horns, and seven crowns upon his heads. And his tail drew the third part of the stars of heaven, and did cast them to the earth: and the dragon stood before the woman which was ready to be delivered, for to devour her child as soon as it was born. And she brought forth a man child, who was to rule all nations with a rod of iron: and her child was caught up unto God, and to his throne. And the woman fled into the wilderness, where she hath a place prepared of god, that they should feed her there a thousand two hundred and threescore days. And there was a war in heaven: Michael and his angels fought against the dragon; and the dragon fought and his angels, and prevailed not ... And the great dragon was cast out, that old serpent, called the Devil, and Satan ... into the earth ... Therefore rejoice, ye heavens, and ye that dwell in them. Woe to the inhabitors of the earth and of the sea ... And when the dragon saw that he was cast unto the earth, he persecuted the woman which brought forth the manchild. And to the woman were given two wings of a great eagle, that she might fly into the wilderness, into her place, where she is nourished for a time, and times, and half a time, from the face of the serpent. And the serpent cast out of his mouth water as a flood after the woman, that he might cause her to be carried away of the flood. And the earth helped the woman, and the earth opened her mouth, and swallowed up the flood which the red dragon cast out of his mouth. And the dragon ... went to make war with the remnant of her seed which keep the commandments of God and have the testimony of Jesus Christ.

This text is about a truly powerful female spiritual archetype. It is deliberately ambiguous and within it can be found many interpretations, all of which are controversial within our current paternalistic interpretations of the Judaic/Christian stories. Is this the story of the Virgin Mary and the birth of Jesus Christ, his persecution, death and legacy? Is it the ongoing battle between Christianity and the Devil? Is it the real story of Eve, of the fall of man and its ensuing curse (in other words, a menstrual allegory)? If instead, the woman is Mary, then do we assume that menstruation arrived with us at the same time as Jesus? Or is the woman the earth set within the planets and the sun and moon of our own solar system? Is it mankind becoming mortal, devolving from its immortal and seemingly happy cousins in heaven from where the woman and the dragon appear? Is this a secondary cataclysm after the great flood spoken of in many cultures' scriptures, a meteorite bombardment bringing climatic change and engendering new life forms or accelerating evolution? The child born might be Adam, the first man, as well as Jesus Christ, or perhaps Moses. Whatever the case, he is born of woman. The interpretation is directly reliant on the reader but seems to be referring to older, lost notions of a more diverse and ambiguous deity.

If you compare St John's vision to Milton's *Paradise Lost* (which, like Revelations, is both a political as well as spiritual text) with its hurling out of Satan from heaven and his pursuit of Adam and Eve to Eden, it aligns more effectively. Although Milton was deeply Christian he deals comfortably with notions of angels, demons and demigods. This approach relates quite happily with those found in the classical texts of Rome and Greece, and is perhaps even an acknowledgement of these works. In Milton the deities are able to reproduce asexually, a linking factor with the behaviour of Eastern and Egyptian goddesses and gods. Satan, then Lucifer, the angel of light, fantasises so fervently about his ideal lover that she comes to life and is born from his head: her name is Sin. Satan then rapes her, and she gives birth to a child, Death. Having committed sexual violence and incest which produce horrific consequences, Satan is then cast out of heaven by Michael, as described in Revelations.

So many possible interpretations and allegorical potentials present themselves to the varied social and historical mindsets of the audiences of these texts. Similarities often appear. An initial being (the atom) is somehow cleft in two. One of the offspring is male, one female, both from the same initial being; they are therefore the same and together they make the sum of the whole; neither one is better than the other.

The use and translation of language is at its root divisive; it is the flip side of progress. 'Truth' is layered in the parables and stories from other eras. Man and mankind: the words seem similar, yet the first is gender specific, whilst the second is a collective noun for all men and women. Active female priests have been somewhat written out of the books.

Religion does not escape dogma. Once it has been transcribed, it becomes a most powerful secular tool. It is important to see who was writing what and when. Below is a chart taken from the Church of England's *Alpha Manual*. It is used as proof of Jesus Christ's physical existence and is based on how many original texts still exist.

| Work | Date of writing | Earliest copy | No. of original remaining copies |
| --- | --- | --- | --- |
| Herodotus | 488–428 BC | AD 900 | 8 |
| Thucydides | 460–400 BC | AD 900 | 8 |
| Tacitus | AD 100 | AD 1100 | 20 |
| Caesar's *Gallic Wars* | 58–50 BC | AD 900 | 9–10 |
| Livy's *Roman History* | 59–17 BC | AD 900 | 20 |
| New Testament | AD 40–100 | AD 350 | 5,000 Greek 10,000 Latin 9,300 others |

The difference in the numbers is quite extraordinary. Bear in mind too that each copy would have had to have been hand copied in a time before the printing press – surely a hugely expensive project. Who paid for it? It is likely that the most widely available editions would be the ones that had been allowed or encouraged to survive and were thus the most agreeable to the authorities, faced with a socialist religious revolution. Conversely, it is possible that the most threatening and powerful books were deliberately destroyed. History bears witness to countless desecrations and book burnings – the demons of the present are the gods of the past. The versions we are left with are overwhelmingly paternalistic in language and structure, culminating in an all-male Trinity, contradictory to most examples in science and nature.

The Bible seems to be a manual for how men should behave better. Where is the book for the bettering of women? Much of women's history and ritual is passed down orally. Historically this has often been against a background of oppression and war. In the Americas, for instance, the histories of entire clans were kept alive by the women, simply because the majority of men (priests and warriors especially) were killed. Similarly, the emancipation of women in the United Kingdom in the twentieth century was greatly advanced by the First and Second World Wars, when women had to do 'men's work' due to the absence of the men on the home front.

Women have their icons: Cleopatra, Virgin Mary, Boadicea, Joan of Arc, St Brigid, the Queen of Sheba, Sheherazade, Ruth and Kali. But where is the daughter of God? The female spirit? The female Pope? We are left with fairies, Mary Magdalene and Mother Earth – passive, pretty, whoring and providing. Furthermore, women are (if they are not the passive kind) sexualised and demonised, often by their own blood. The point of menstruation is fertility and giving life – in fact, creation. Yet, unlike the blood of Christ, it is widely tabooed as unclean and dirty. In many male initiation rites, however, blood-letting and blood imagery is central, possibly emulating menstruation as the entry into adult life. Menstruation has not been fully understood for so long that it has become feared; women have been taught to fear their bodies.

Science has equally neglected women. In 1957 *Sexual Deviations in the Female*, a Freudian analysis by Louis Samuel London, stated confidently that a female patient who wished to buy her boyfriend a drink (and indeed expressed a wish to pay independently on several occasions) was of course a latent homosexual. She was naturally prescribed tranquillisers for her unhappy condition! How far from the ducking stool have we come? A woman can still be used to topple empires with sex.

# Genetics and race

Some Australian Aboriginal peoples believe that we are all evolving from our mixture of global colours back to one original colour: brown. (Interestingly although these Aborigines mark the arrival of Christ on the planet, they claim that he did not come to them because they were already living according to the way of the spirit, at one with the soul of the land.) Race, rather like gender, is one of the most physically obvious, but intrinsically manipulative, aspects of mankind. Ironically, although race is one of the most immediately striking differences, it is also one of the most genetically superficial. There is far less genetic difference between individuals of different races than between those of different gender. The story of the Tower of Babel in the Old Testament states that we were originally one race, divided as a punishment by God to prevent us from regaining heaven.

Tolmec and Mayan carvings depict African and European faces, and their legends speak of fair skinned, white- or yellow-haired gods from across the sea. Thor Heyerdahl proved that people could cross the Atlantic, and recent archaelogical finds in Oregon controversially confirmed this genetic diversity when a 9,300-year-old skeleton was found to have European-type DNA.

We have genetic proof that every one of us is related at some point in human history, whether it be 20,000 or 220,000 years ago. The red herring of race has been used to divide the work-force, using the basic economic premise that if you can divide people into classes, you can pay them differently. This has paved the way for general social inequality. It is a secular issue of money, property and land (and thus, also agriculture and food); it has little to do with individuals and their physical differences.

Luckily for politicians, it is also easy to exploit, as survival of the fittest is an underlying trend in evolution. Despite race and gender issues being almost completely focused on the material level, many religions cling to notions of chosen peoples. Stereotypes rage constantly through time, wearing the aesthetic guises of fashions and epochs. You only have to read Shakespeare's works such as *Othello, The Merchant of Venice, The Taming of the Shrew* and *Romeo and Juliet* to see that there is very little new in these prejudiced and divisive reactions to perceived difference.

Within both religion and politics, how we communicate – the languages we use – is central to functioning within the collective, and ultimately to individual, survival. This is glaringly obvious when, for example, you drive three hours west out of London, leaving behind the 'Lahnden' accent and arriving at the sing-song Welsh. These local dialects of the same spoken language are completely different. It is surprising that such small geographical differences can create so great a difference in basic group behaviour and identity. Yet, it is something we expect, and is further proof of the staggering levels of conditioning regarding gender, race and sexuality. How you speak is a completely learned behaviour. This is the paradox of identity: we all desire to be part of the collective, to function within a group, yet, by denying the impact of social conditioning regarding gender, race and, often, sexuality, we fracture the greater collective of humanity.

## Paradox

Where we would once have looked to the spirit, science now looks more and more to genetics for answers. Yet scientists still chase the touchstone of all religions, immortality, just as their predecessors, the alchemists, did; they are still trying to replicate creation. In the context of genetics the story of Noah's ark springs to my mind. Scholars seem pretty much agreed that there was a great flood and the Noah version of it has always seemed nice. Yet, when we consider the numbers, the billions of species involved, the scale of the ark should be approximately one third of the planet! However, if you had a genetic ark where everything would fit quite compactly in phials and petri dishes, with instructions for its use on a couple of CDs, it is somewhat more conceivable.

Despite our desire to replicate species scientifically, our technological advances are currently stripping the planet of the same number of species of plant and animal life each year. We seem desperate to deny our links to planetary evolution, as if by doing so we can deny our own mortality and the inevitability of change and decay and death.

In our evolutionary development we are physically exactly as we were 30,000 years ago. In one lifetime we go through dramatic physical growth and change: the foetus within the womb assumes, in sequence, all stages of animal evolution on earth, from single cell to fish, to bird, to primate, to human. At some point we are all these things. Genetics has shown us parallels to traditionally primitive ideas of ancestor worship and spirit animal guides. We are all the genetic inheritors of our ancestors; we are all the atavists.

Darwin killed God, just as Christ killed Apollo and the Green Man. Arthur and his Knights of the Round Table echo the Last Supper of Christ and the Apostles – the stories are endlessly confused. Truth and lies are inextricably woven in and out through the aesthetics of our time.

Archetypes fall, paradoxically, directly between instinct and logic, between science fact and science fiction. Whereas stereotypes define our societies, archetypes cut across time, through culture and learnt behaviours, to something instantly recognisable, instantly to our core nature. (Beware, we can be taught to fear them!) Stereotypes are the creation of fashion; archetypes are fashioned after fact, 'the real thing'. These archetypes are the basis of most languages and are the embodiment of the communicative and imaginative abilities. The languages you speak allow you direct access into the areas where you have power. How many languages do you speak?

In my work I use visual languages based on sight. Music is, of course, the sound-based equivalent – both cut across linguistic barriers. For me, painting is a spiritual continuity. With a photograph or film I am consciously aware of a specific capturing of time. I know that a photograph is an image of the past, something which happened over a specific duration, perhaps conveying a specific event. I am aware that the film was then developed and printed: a mechanical intervention, a subtly, yet completely, different kind of process to painting. You cannot know how long it takes a painting or sculpture to evolve. There is no specific time to engender the idea, no definitive technique to construct or develop the image. The viewer of a painting, unlike the viewer of a photograph, will have no concept of time. I am constantly being asked how long a work of art has taken me to produce. People want to know because they cannot calculate it.

Both film and painting intend to capture the living memory. The former is perceived as real (often, in reality, it is not) and viewed literally; the latter, no matter how realistically it is rendered, is seen as metaphysical. When I am painting, the connection between myself and the image is me; with a camera or computer I am slightly distanced and protected by the tool I am using. At first glance it may appear very similar, but the process with the paintbrush is far less safe, for I am fundamentally and intrinsically dealing in illusions, conjuring the three-dimensional out of the two-dimensional. It is a cheap trick of perception and eyesight; I make a mark on the surface and it becomes something different. Yet, it is a truth. The image is important socially and historically because looking at painting is like looking into a mirror: it is reality, but completely physically unreal. It is an attempt to communicate that reality.

Mirrors, paintings and sight are all based on light. Light, usually in the form of the sun or fire, or some aspect of the divine light (haloes or auras), is fundamental to most religions. I am again chasing the intangible, the anti-reductionist dream: the belief that we are all atomically linked and that we have basic physical requirements, light being one of them. If this is the case I will instinctively be drawn to images and imaging.

What drives humankind into the twenty-first century? Have the underlying instincts and impulses changed? No, they are, as always, food, sex, greed and fear, and love. The catalysts and triggers for these impulses, however, constantly change. The rate at which they change seems to be accelerating, with genetically engineered food as a prime example.

The basic survival requirement is food. Most religions at source level are constructed around a geographic and an agricultural environment. Doctrines often include strict dietary guidelines. Food has always carried both spiritual and commercial values, as it is concerned with land and property and it has a sacramental use in religious rituals.

However, greed is now packaged to extreme limits. We live in an exceptionally decadent age, a surreal consumer society: Midas, Nero and Genghis Khan all rolled into one. How does it sell? Image and advertising. Again, this is nothing new in nature: he with the brightest feathers wins the bird. But the speed and quantity of information received and transmitted by the medium of televsion and the internet has not been experienced previously. Information technology would seem to be the new global language for the millennium.

Yet more paradoxes are diet foods (foods with the food taken out). There are weight-watchers in the northern hemisphere and starvation in the southern hemisphere. There are magazines, books and television programmes devoted solely to the choice and preparation of foods – a surfeit of gourmet delights. Whilst on the other channel, you can watch emaciated infants, orphaned, injured and left to die. None of it seems real.

Then we have contraception: diet sex (sex with the reproduction taken out). Sex sells, and so we are constantly asked to choose, define and redefine sexual tastes and lifestyles in the most mundane areas of our lives. It seems that we no longer want children, selfishly preferring instead to live longer ourselves. Yet, the sexual appetite manifests itself as strongly as ever.

Both food and sex are archetypal, but both have taboo elements and aspects, cannibalism and incest for example. Yet one of the least addressed taboos in the West is death. Whilst we seem to be desperately trying to increase our longevity, we cannot fail to realise that we have in fact sold out to the consumer patriarchy. We consider ourselves to be powerless as individuals on the global scale, yet see that we are obsessed with making life (fuelled by genetics and survival fears). It seems that our fears of survival as a species are also accelerating. There is a definite dialogue between archetypes and taboos: taboos are generally the suppressed, or evil, archetypes of the era.

Here, it seems, we need religious instruction. However, religion cannot compete with television or consumerism; although it may use both. Spirituality is often unseen, while we rely more and more on the television screen to inform us about our needs and desires. Technology runs on unseen electricity and vibrations with light on a subatomic level. The human psyche is bombarded with moving images. It yearns for stills, for intimate dialogue, for self-investigation and contemplation. Whereas the television takes us out of ourselves, the un-moving image provides a meditation; it scrutinises the moment and ignores time; it accesses intuition, empathy and emotion. We store away images from the moment we are born. From crucifixes to Coca Cola logos, image is crucial. The power of signs and symbols still directs humankind. We are, after all, only a series of electrical impulses closely associated with, but physically unconnected to, our bodies – another paradox.

# Rowena Shepherd – the author

# The house of dreams

The power behind the Tarot cards is the timeless use of images as powerful tools to contact a higher or greater reality, a reality which links us all together and which sparks off dreams and ideas from our subconscious. As Cynthia Giles points out in her book, *Tarot: The Complete Guide*, the power of the archetypal image was approached anew in the twentieth century through the ideas of the psychologist Carl Jung.

During the second half of the twentieth century, Carl Jung was the central influence on occultism in general, and certainly on the study of Tarot. His theory of the 'archetypal unconscious' – a reservoir of imaginative knowledge shared by all human kind, and expressing itself in recognisable ways through the imagery of art, dream and vision – has become the basis for a new, and, in many respects, more sound, approach to the nature and symbolism of the Tarot.

Dreams and the physical image have thus become interchangeable in their use in the Tarot cards. Over time, the images on them have become layered with the mystical and allegorical symbols of the times through which they have passed, distilling them into potent archetypes.

The cards' power is authenticated, not just by their ancient origins, but also by their continual reinvention, without which the images would become meaningless. Sally Annett's Tarot cards follow this tradition. She has distilled her own life experiences and meditational inspiration following Crowley's deck of cards and re-created them in her time for her generation. The key to her cards, like Crowley's, is the Aeon card (Crowley's invention). This card described Crowley's vision of the future; and in Sally's cards it is this simple, yet powerful, image which is the core of her own philosophy.

The divinatory method of laying out the cards into structures, in turn translates the images into a structure we can relate to our Newtonian world. The concept underlying the format of this book is that each layout of the cards for telling fortunes creates a visual house of images. This is similar to the Renaissance concept of the theatre of memory described by Frances Yates in her book, *The Art of Memory*, where visual symbols representing varied ideas are placed around an imagined theatre or tableau. A person enters this theatre of memory whenever they wish to bring to mind the ideas represented. Thus, the cards create a house of images which, when laid out in a particular schema, interrelate in such a way as to create resonances providing clues to the narrative patterns within each person's life story.

Our minds work in a linear narrative way. We stand at each reading in the room marked Present, around us are doors that open out on to our Future and Past possibilities and our hopes and fears around the issues affecting us in the present. As we move through space and time the different positions shift and our perception of who we are and what we wish for, or are afraid of, changes. The only constant is change. By exploring this process through the cards we can start to break down some of the linear nature of our understanding of our existence, and thus see the patterns that reoccur and challenge us in our current life.

# Science and the Tarot

Contemporary science is currently split into quantum and Newtonian physics. We live our lives based on Newtonian physics: gravity pulls matter downwards, time moves in a linear fashion and objects move through space in predictable ways. However, quantum physics has a much more chaotic structure, almost predictable through its unpredictability. Subatomic particles seem to teleport from one place in space-time to a completely unrelated part of space-time; many universes can exist within our experience of one universe. Our existence is in fact not linked with time at all. Our past and present and future can happen in any order and at the same time; our future is an influence on our past as much as our past has an effect on our future.

This clash between the so-called real world, as perceived by our physical senses and rational minds and represented by Newtonian physics, and that of the unperceived, hidden or obscured realities, which exist alongside and are represented by quantum physics, is not in itself new. It could be likened to a clash in the Renaissance between the socially acceptable reality of the powerful élites and the hidden beliefs and political views of the less powerful majority (and, of course, of those experimenting with the occult or hidden philosophies of a magic-science).

# The wise Fool

This theme of hidden political messages can be found in early literature related to the archetypal images on Tarot cards. Teofilo Folengo's poem (see page 208) was created from 'reading' Tarot cards in the order in which they were laid out. The fact that the cards were laid out according to fate allowed the poet telling the stories from the cards, Limeruno, to speak his mind. As he did this he allied himself with the Fool card. This indicated that whatever he were to say could not be taken seriously as it was foolish, thus protecting Limeruno from any recriminations.

This concept of the politically subversive Fool can also be found in the tradition of the humorous and ribald stories popular in the mid-1490s.

These included such tales as Boccaccio's *Decameron* and indeed Chaucer's *Canterbury Tales*. The following is a synopsis of the first tale from a collection of *novelle* known as *Le Porretane,* written by the Bolognese author Giovanni Sabadino degli Arienti, and which was apparently presented to the Duke of Ferrara.

In 1475 a group of upper-class Bolognese travelled to the baths at Poretta with Andrea Bentivoglio, a cousin of the despot of Bologna, Giovanni II Bentivoglio. One of their company was the nobleman and soldier, Annibale da Caglia. One day they settled by a stream and determined to amuse themselves by telling stories.

Seeing an old man walk by muttering to the plants and flowers, Annibale da Caglia related an amusing event concerning Triunfo da Camerino, a groom employed by Piero delli Ubaldini, a gentleman from Urbino. Triunfo had requested an hour off every day, which, due to his abilities, he was granted by Ubaldini. So, every day having completed his duties, he retired to his room and locked it. There he hung a curtain on his wall, on which he painted the Pope and his cardinals in consistory, and many kings, princes, lords and dukes.

Triunfo then placed himself before the depiction in the place of the Emperor, wearing a crown and holding a sceptre and impersonating the Pope (despite his dress). He began to address his painted congregation, urging them to make peace amongst themselves in order to better attack the Turks. He then assumed the person of the Emperor and addressed the Pope, recalling a dream (he had had as Emperor) of the devil and urging the Pope to set a better example to his people. He would then proceed, with a leap and a shout, to talk of military matters, finally fencing in front of the depiction. He then replied in the name of kings, princes and lords, before placing 'the world' (presumably his orb, although this is not made clear) upside down in his arms, and making the concluding address. Thus he spent about an hour every day, before returning to his work in the stables.

Triunfo's behaviour aroused Ubaldini's curiosity, and one day he spied on him through a crack in the wall. Ubaldini was so amused at what he saw that he burst out laughing and called several friends – a soldier, commander and a courtier – to watch. Then calling Triunfo before him, Ubaldini congratulated him on his elevation from groom to emperor. He asked that Triunfo commend him to fortune, who had placed Triunfo at the summit of her wheel. Triunfo, deeply embarrassed, immediately tore down his painted curtain, folded it up and left Ubaldini's household and the city. Nobody knew where he went.

This story is clearly intended to mock Triunfo da Camerino's delusions of grandeur and his foolish behaviour. However, it is clear that underlying the humorous nature of this tale is revealed the political mistrust of the upper ruling classes by the lower and their frustration at not being able to change or effect events, although Sabadino would have been shocked at such a suggestion. Triunfo has no power to control events; he does not live in a democracy; and he is angry at the events which he sees taking place. So he becomes the Emperor and Pope in order to role-play his feelings and anger. As soon as he is spied upon by his master, he becomes the Fool.

The significance of this tale is that it was written during the time when the *trionfi* or Tarot cards were becoming popular and that it was composed in the city state of Bologna where the cards appear to have been created. It is interesting that some of the archetypes referred to in the groom's images are the same as those we find on Tarot cards, and indeed that the groom's name was Triunfo, close to *trionfi,* the name for the cards at the time.

I do not believe that it is a coincidence that the Fool card of the Tarot appears to be the most important. Traditionally fools were often people of such a low class that they would have had no influence or ability to communicate with a king. But in their role as fool, they have always had the freedom to say the politically unthinkable to kings. Indeed, they have had a certain interchangeability with the monarchs in classical and medieval literature and mystic tales. In classical and medieval tales asses' ears were worn both by kings and fools. Examples of this can be found in King Midas and in the fool who became an ass in the magical tale of the Golden Ass (which was based on the initiation ceremonies to the cult of Isis). A sixteenth-century saying explained the unique status of kings and fools by pointing out that one can be born a king or a fool, but can never attain either of these positions.

In a sense, like Limeruno in Folengo's sonnet, by reading the Tarot cards, we ally ourselves with the Fool card in that we are doing something which seems quite foolish. Yet, this foolishness allows us the freedom to comment on the way in which people live their lives, and in such a way that even one's best friends would not be allowed. Being the Fool when reading Tarot cards also allows us to break through the Newtonian concepts of perceived, rational understanding of the world and to reveal hidden underlying truths it would otherwise seem foolish to believe in.

# THE LIBRARY

## Bibliography

◆

### Tarot reading

**Anthony, Louis.** *Tarot, Plain and Simple,* Llewellyn Publications, Minnesota, 1998
A straightforward and practical approach to the divinatory interpretation of the cards, using a version of the Rider–Waite deck created by Robin Wood.

**Case, Paul Foster.** *The Tarot: A Key to the Wisdom of the Ages,* BOTA Ltd, Los Angeles, 1990
An early, and fundamental book in the American occult cannon. It studies the magical imagery of the cards in a intelligible way, introducing modern psychology in its approach. It uses Case's version of the Rider–Waite deck.

**Crowley, Aleister.** *The Book of Thoth,* Samuel Weiser Inc., Maine, 1996 (originally published 1969)
The book which accompanied Crowley's Tarot pack; a rich, if dense, guide to the magical symbolism used in his cards.

**Hamaker-Zondag, Karen.** *The Way of the Tarot,* Judy Piatkus Ltd, London, 1998
A Jungian approach to working with the Tarot cards, using the Rider–Waite deck.

**Pollack, Rachel.** *Seventy-Eight Degrees of Wisdom,* Thorsons, London, 1997
A readable and detailed approach to the divinatory meanings of the cards, rooted in the Rider–Waite deck.

**Waite, Arthur Edward.** *A Pictorial Key to the Tarot,* William Rider & Son, London, 1910
Waite's own guide to using the Rider–Waite deck. It is perhaps more of historical interest than of practical use for reading the cards, because it is written in a highly stylised manner. But it provides an insight into the origins of the use of today's Tarot, and also of the personal conflicts in belief held by Waite and other occultists.

**Zeigler, Gerd.** *Tarot: Mirror of the Soul,* Samuel Weiser Inc., Maine, 1988
An accessible and essential book for anyone interested in studying, or using, Crowley's Thoth deck.

# Tarot history

**Arienti, Giovanni Sabadino degli.** *Le Porretane,* edited by Bruno
Basile, Salerno Editrice, Rome, 1981
A collection of amusing Italian Renaissance short stories, in the tradition
of Boccaccio's *Decameron.* The first story provides an interesting insight
into the use of archetypal images similar to those on Tarot cards.

**Calvino, Italo.** *The Castle of Crossed Destinies,* translated by William
Weaver, Vintage, London, 1997
A novel using the Visconti Sforza and Marseille Tarot decks as visual
clues to a story. It is written in the romance tradition of the Italian
Renaissance.

**Christian, Paul.** *Le Homme rouge des Tuileries,* Paris, 1863
Primarily a book on divination with astrology. However, he introduces
his complex system, related to the Rosy Cross, linking the Tarot cards to
astrology. It also includes an invented version of an Egyptian initiation
ceremony, with Tarot cards as its base.

**Court de Gébelin, Antoine.** *Monde primitif, analysé et comparé avec le
monde moderne,* Paris, 1781, Volume 8
In this eight-volume work, Court de Gébelin published some of the
knowledge and beliefs of French occult secret societies. In the last
volume he brings in the Tarot cards, suggesting that they had Egyptian
origins. He also publishes the Comte de Mellet's essay on the cards, in
which they are linked to the Qabalah for the first time.

**Decker, Ronald, Depaulis, Thierry and Dummett, Michael.** *A Wicked
Pack of Cards,* Duckworth Ltd, London, 1996
A rigorous and academic examination of the history of the Tarot cards,
with an excellent critique of the personalities behind the Tarot myths. It
is heavily slanted to the belief that the cards were merely playing cards
the use of which was subverted by misguided pseudo-magicians.

**Etteilla.** *Etteilla, ou instructions sur l'art de tirer les cartes. Troisième et
dernière édition.* Segault and Legras, Amsterdam and Paris, 1783
Etteilla's instructions for fortune-telling with cards. These contain his
description of the origins of *The Book of Thoth*, or Tarot cards, along
with their mystical meanings.

**Giles, Cynthia.** *Tarot: The Complete Guide,* Robert Hale, London, 1993
This book contains an excellent run-through of the history of the cards.
It also attempts to look at why the cards might work, using
contemporary science to explain the possibilities.

**Hall, Manly Palmer.** *An Encyclopedic Outline of Masonic, Hermetic,
Qabalistic and Rosicrucian Symbolical Philosophy,* M. P. Hall, San
Francisco, 1928
As the title suggests, this is an encyclopedic and indispensable examination
of occult and magical symbolism, although it is now a little dated.

**Hind, A. M.** *Early Italian Engravings,* Quaritch, London, 1938–48, Volume 1
The classic work on the attribution of early Italian engravings.

**Kaplan, Stuart R.** *The Encyclopedia of Tarot,* US Games Systems Inc., New York, 1978–86, Volumes 1–3
An encyclopedic, if idiosyncratic, examination of the history of Tarot cards. However, because of its coverage, it is indispensable to any serious collector of Tarot cards or student of the history of the Tarot cards.

**Knight, Gareth.** *Treasure House of Images,* The Aquarian Press, Wellingborough, 1986
A fair examination of the history of the Tarot cards. What makes this book worth reading is the author's approach to the iconography of the cards and their use in path-working with the Qabalah.

**Lévi, Éliphas.** *Histoire de la Magie,* Paris, 1880
The edition of the *History of Magic* in which Lévi suggests that gypsies were involved in the dissemination of Tarot cards in Europe. It also contains a detailed interpretation of the Tarot cards in relation to contemporary occultism.

**Leyden, Rudolf von.** *Ganjifa – the Playing Cards of India,* exhibition catalogue, Victoria and Albert Museum, London, 1982
An exhibition of Indian playing cards, with an academic examination of the development and spread of playing cards from China to Europe.

**Moakley, Gertrude.** *The Tarot Cards Painted by Bembo,* New York Public Library, 1966
An interesting art historical approach to the images on early Italian Tarot cards. The author proposes that the images were linked to Petrarch's *Triumphs* and contemporary festival processions. However, some of her suggestions are now seen as flawed in the light of later research.

**Molfino, Anna Mottola and Mauro Natale.** *Le Muse e il Principe, Arte di corte nel Rinascimento Padano,* exhibition catalogue, Museo Poldi Pezzoli, Milan, 1991
An exhibition on the art created for the Renaissance court of Padua. It includes a complete set of colour images of the Sola Busci Tarot deck.

**Morley, H. T.** *Old and Curious Playing Cards,* Bracken Books, London, 1989
A dated, but well-illustrated, guide to the history of playing cards.

**O'Neill, Robert V.** *Tarot Symbolism,* Fairways Press, 1986
A carefully reasoned, but dated, academic approach to the history of the esoteric side of the Tarot. His understanding of the Renaissance is flawed by an over-estimation of the influence of esoteric and mystical beliefs on Renaissance man. However, it is a good antidote to the Decker, Depaulis and Dummett book.

**Ovid.** *Metamorphoses,* edited and translated by E. J. Kenny and A. D. Melville, Oxford, 1998, Book 1
The classic text on the original idea of the Golden Age.

**Papus.** *The Tarot of the Bohemians,* translated by A. P. Morgan, Senate, London, 1994
This book is interesting from the historical point of view because of its proposal that the gypsies were the originators of the Tarot cards. It also updates much of Lévi and Paul Christian's ideas, and adds the author's own version of the relationship of the cards to astrology.

**Petrarch, Francesco.** *The Triumphs of Francesco Petrarch,* translated by Henry Boyd, John Murray, London and Cambridge, Mass., 1906
Petrarch's collection of sonnets based on his unrequited passion for Laura, which inspired many other works of art and literature in the Renaissance.

**Pratesi, Francesco.** *'Italian Cards: New Discoveries no. 2',* The Playing Card, Vol. XV, 1987, pp. 26–36
An interesting, if variable, discussion of the meanings and ordering of the Tarot triumphs written by a Piedmontese author in the sixteenth century.

**Pratesi, Francesco.** *'Italian Cards: New Discoveries, no. 9'.* The Playing Card, Vol. XVII, 1989, pp.136–45
An anonymous and very interesting relation of the meanings and ordering of the Tarot triumphs, found in the Library of the University of Bologna, and dated to the sixteenth century.

**Regardie, Israel.** *The Golden Dawn, Volumes 1 and 2,* Llewellyn Publications, Minnesota, 1974
Regardie's edited personal copy of the Golden Dawn's Knowledge papers.

**Sheperd, J.** *The Tarot Trumps,* Aquarian Press, Wellingborough, 1985
A short and digestible approach to the history of the cards.

**Vaillant, Jean-Alexandre.** *Les Rômes, Histoire vraie des vrais Bohémiens,* E. Dentu, Paris, 1857
This volume contains the author's version of the Tarot cards' dissemination into Europe via the gypsies, including his understanding of their mythological origins. A difficult read because of his creative reconstruction of the cards' origins using a mixture of half-understood mythologies and the similarities of the sounds of words in different cultures.

**Weston, Jesse Laidlay.** *From Ritual to Romance,* Princeton University Press, Princeton, 1993
An influential and useful book, although it has now been academically discredited. It examines the links between the Tarot suits, the four Grail Hallows and the Celtic treasures of Ireland.

# Qabalah

**Ashcroft-Nowicki, Dolores.** *The Shining Paths,* Aquarian Press, Wellingborough, 1983
A collection of magical path-workings based on the thirty-two paths of the Qabalistic Tree of Life. It is an excellent starting point for meditating on the Qabalah, which continues to be a rich source of inspiration for the occult student.

**Ashcroft-Nowicki, Dolores.** *The Ritual Magic Workbook – A Practical Course of Self-Initiation,* Aquarian Press, London, 1986
An excellent starting point for anyone wishing to learn ritual magic. It is full of practical exercises, using the Qabalah and magic in the Western occult tradition.

**Butler, W. E.** *Apprenticed to Magic and Magic and the Qabalah,* Aquarian Press, Wellingborough, 1990
A good point of departure for the student of occult studies who wishes to further their understanding of magic and the Qabalah.

**Fortune, Dion.** *The Mystical Qabalah,* Aquarian Press, London, 1987
A detailed examination of the various meanings of the Sephiroth on the Tree of Life. It is written in a format that makes it a usable reference book for both the beginner and expert.

**Knight, Gareth.** *A Practical Guide to Qabalistic Symbolism,* Helios Publications Ltd, Toddington, 1965, Volumes 1 and 2
An early and fundamental approach to the subject. The first volume contains a detailed analysis of the symbolism related to the thirty-two paths of the Tree of Life. The second volume goes on to relate the Qabalah to the Tarot cards.

**Wang, Robert.** *The Quabalistic Tarot,* Samuel Weiser Inc., York Beach, Maine, 1987 (originally published 1983)
A detailed and important analysis of the way in which the Tarot cards relate to the Qabalah.

# Other reading

*The Bible*
I am not going to suggest any particular version of the Bible, or any specific chapters, because as a whole this is obviously one of the most important and influential texts for Western religion and spirituality.

**Billington, Sandra.** *A Social History of the Fool,* Harvester Press, Brighton, 1982.
A fascinating insight into the role of the Fool in English Society c. 1220–1896.

**Burnley, David.** *The History of the English Language,* Longman Higher Education, 1992
A good grounding in the study of linguistics in relation to the English language.

**Byron, George.** *Don Juan,* University of Texas Press, Austin, 1957
Mock-epic poem encompassing universal themes of love, politics, passion and satire.

**Hagger, Nicholas.** *The Universe and the Light,* Element Books Ltd, Dorset, 1993
An interesting metaphysical look at contemporary cosmology.

**Jung, Carl Gustave.** *Man and His Symbols,* Aldus Books, London, 1964
An opportunity to introduce yourself to the ideas of Jung.

**Lewin, Roger.** *'Young Americans',* New Scientist, 17 October 1998, pp. 24–28
An article examining the controversy surrounding recent research on the ethnic origins of prehistoric Americans.

**Lewis Davies, Lyn.** *The Alpha Course Manual,* Cyhoeddiadau'r Gair, 1996
The textbook accompanying the Church of England's introduction course to Christian teachings and living life as a Christian.

**London, Louis Samuel.** *Sexual Deviations in the Female,* Julian Press, New York, 1957
The subtitle 'case histories of frustrated women' describes the slant of this clinical study.

**Matthews, John.** *The Grail Tradition,* Element Books Ltd, Dorset, 1993
A very readable examination of the Grail mythologies.

**Milton, John.** *Paradise Lost,* Penguin, London, 1996
A thought-provoking seventeenth-century version of the fall of man, which read alongside the Bible, and in particular Revelations, reveals a more complex version of Christian mysticism.

**Mountford, Charles, P.** *The Dawn of Time,* Rigby Ltd, Australia, 1974
A retelling of various Aboriginal myths.

**Redgrove, Peter and Shuttle, Penelope.** *'The Wise Wound' Menstruation and Everywoman,* Harper Collins, London, 1994
A thought-provoking examination of the mythological, historical and psychological story of menstruation.

**Roberts, Gareth.** *The Mirror of Alchemy,* The British Library, London, 1994
A comprehensive and academic approach to the history of, and theories behind, the practice of alchemy.

**Yates, Frances.** *The Art of Memory,* Penguin, Harmondsworth, 1969
Although now largely discredited in academic circles, this book still provides a provoking theory on the use of visualisation in the Renaissance.

# Index